"[*Instant Analysis*] cleared up an awful lot for me.... Interesting and very provocative..."

— "Mindy Johnson Show," WMSX-AM/Brockton

"Dr. David Lieberman...has penned a fascinating book.... If you pick up the book, you will start to read about yourself even if you're not willing to admit it. [*Instant Analysis*] demonstrates that changing one's life is simple and doesn't have to take years of therapy."

—Brian Nuthall, CFPL Radio 98, "The Experts," London's News, Talk, and Entertainment/Canada

"If you read Dr. Lieberman's book, you can save yourself countless years [of therapy. *Instant Analysis*] is brilliant. It makes so much sense.... It's a wonderful book and greatly needed."

— "Afternoon Health Show"

"It truly says it all."

— "Author, Author," PBS/Minnesota

"It is a brilliant book.... I was very taken with this.... The book is a very hopeful book...because [Dr. Lieberman] not only defines why we have these habits, but how we can get rid of them or get on the road to getting rid of them very quickly, easily...brief but pointed and accurate."

— "Louise Collins Show," WHWH-AM/Philadelphia

"David Lieberman...has come to the rescue.... He's written a...how-to book on coping with the little things that hang us up most of the time."

— "Afternoon Report," Newschannel 8/Washington, D.C.

INSTANT
ANALYSIS

David J. Lieberman, Ph.D.

ST. MARTIN'S GRIFFIN

New York

Design by Michael Mendelsohn of MISSING MAP Design 2000, Inc.

Library of Congress Cataloging-in-Publication Data

Lieberman, David, J.
    Instant analysis / David J. Lieberman.
        p.   cm.
    ISBN 0-312-19466-8
    1. Self-defeating behavior.   2. Change (Psychology)   I. Title
    BF637.S37L45   1997   97-8968
    158.1—dc21   CIP

First St. Martin's Griffin Edition: September 1998

10 9 8 7 6 5 4 3 2 1

CONTENTS

PART TWO: IT ISN'T OVER YET

ACKNOWLEDGMENTS

I WOULD LIKE to acknowledge all those who, through the years, have placed their wellness in my hands. You have fueled my desire to write this book and ignited in me a life-long purpose. I am grateful for this privilege.

Most certainly I am thankful for the love, guidance, and wisdom of my mother and father. And for the unique insights and contributions offered to me by my brothers, Adam and Andrew, I am eternally grateful.

I wish to express my appreciation for Jennifer Enderlin's boundless energy and enthusiasm for this project. Her tireless and passionate efforts, and those of her collegues at St. Martin's Press, are evident throughout this book.

INTRODUCTION

I WROTE THIS BOOK after recognizing the sad fact that many people have to motivate themselves to become excited about their own lives. There's dullness instead of intensity and numbness in place of excitement. They are tired—mentally and physically drained. This is not living. This book is for those who want to put *life* back into their lives.

After countless seminars, lectures, interviews, and conversations, an interesting truth has revealed itself to me. Most people are *almost* happy. They're so close to being the kinds of people they want to be, living the kinds of lives they want to live, yet they are stuck in a mental rut.

I realized that these people seem to share a common challenge—living has become automatic, a dead process. They try to move forward to get well, but no amount of willpower, motivation, unwavering determination, or discipline can change what is not alive.

If you're not the person you would like to be or if you're not living the kind of life you want to be living, it's likely that your life has been reduced to a network of conditioned responses, encased in a cocoon of ideals, habits, fears, and beliefs. You may be alive, but there's no freshness, no vitality. You move through life, but you're not living it.

Focusing on aspects of yourself infuses vitality into your life, so that it's no longer automatic. If you were unconscious, you would not feel the pain of a cut. But if you were awake, you would feel the discomfort and seek to stop the cause instantly. It's not that you want to cause yourself pain, but you are not always aware of the significance of your actions. Just as you need to be alert to physical harm, you need to be consciously aware of psychological pain.

My research has led me to approximately one hundred behaviors that to varying degrees and in various combinations form the structure of automatic thinking. These are the behaviors that keep you from reaching your highest human potential and prevent you from getting the most out of yourself and your life. By becoming fully aware of your unhealthy behaviors, thoughts, and beliefs, you no longer act out of habit. Awareness of the suffering wakes you up, and the automatic network begins to dissolve.

Through a five-phase process, this book shows you how to break free of conditioned living. When your thinking is not mechanical, your actions are fresh. Awareness breathes life into your actions—habits lose their hold and are easily eliminated because your thinking is not mechanical.

You will learn how to take control of your life by breaking free of fixed thought patterns, attitudes, perceptions, beliefs, and behaviors. *Instant Analysis* shows you how to live instead of reacting with preconditioned thinking; you will learn how to "think before you think."

Get ready to live.

INSTANT
ANALYSIS

PART ONE

TIME TO GET BETTER

T HE TICKING OF A CLOCK. If you're not paying attention, it doesn't bother you. However, if you turn your attention to it, all you can hear is the ticking. You realize how annoying it is—so much so that you can't think or concentrate on anything else. But once it moves outside your field of awareness, because you have gotten used to it, it no longer bothers you. You may often have noticed that the muscles in your neck and shoulders are tense. You didn't realize that you were hunching your shoulders, but now when you turn your attention to your body, you become aware of the pain and can simply relax the muscle and ease the tension.

The strength of your shell—this network of behaviors—comes from its power of invisibility. You're unaware of the very actions that create it. By becoming aware of your behavior, thoughts, and feelings, you make visible the process and gain the ability to see the harm.

The objective is to break up your mental routine and break free from conditioned thought patterns. This is accomplished by looking objectively at specific behaviors that usually go unnoticed or unexamined. As you begin to question these behaviors, you will get in the "habit" of not being in the habit.

You can't see yourself directly because not only has your life become mechanical, but you're a part of your own shell. There's no perspective—you're a piece of your own puzzle. Just as it's not possible to see your entire physical self directly, you can only see your psychological self in the reflection of your behaviors. Since direct introspection is difficult, these one hundred behaviors are designed to initiate the process of tearing at the fabric of habitual thinking—cutting away the clutter so you can see yourself objectively.

This book contains one hundred insulation, projection, filtering, and reflection responses. They are called *responses* because they are mechanisms used to respond—to a discrepancy in your life that you are unable or unwilling to acknowledge. They encase you and feed on your fears. They are, in fact, the army of the false self. All of your beliefs, feelings, thoughts, ideas, and fears manifest into a myriad of behaviors. And these ordinary behaviors can reveal the most extraordinary motivations. By seeing yourself in the echo of your activities, you slow the response machine, helping to bring your life to a new level of awareness.

The opinion you hold of yourself today greatly reflects the experiences of your past. These influences, which may have been less than positive, set into motion your network of habits, thoughts, attitudes, and beliefs that remain consistent with your low self-concept. Now you will be able to see the full impact and significance of your self-image on your behaviors—and the self-inflicted wounds that they cause.

Some responses are quite common, due in part to our culture and to human nature. Still, this is not to say that they're not harmful. Some responses suggest not-so-normal and unusual behavior, and they can all occur in varying degrees with a wide range of impact. Most responses have multiple causes, and you may identify with one, some, all, or none.

These responses are the plaque that collects on and distorts your true self and widens the gap between yourself and reality. They also create a breeding ground for more serious illness. The more automated your life is—the more responses that have become integrated into your personality—the wider the gap between reality and your perception of reality, moving you farther into your *own little world*.

Most serious mental illnesses can find their root in this very gap.

Once you acknowledge and understand an aspect of your personality, you're able to see yourself as separate from the shell—"the real you" versus your facade. It's the awareness that drives a wedge into the mechanics of the behavior. Once you see the real you, that part of the shell becomes pointless because the purpose of it was to keep you from self-discovery. The incentive is the same as that of a bald man who wears a toupee in front of those who know that he's bald and whom he wishes not to deceive. There's just no point to it.

By looking at aspects of the self, you slowly chop away at the facade. As each response is exposed, you get closer to the actual self, until the barrier no longer exists. Small cracks in the shell appear as you begin to expose more of your true self. Then the shell simply dissolves and your true self emerges fearless and confident. You will begin to understand why you do what you do, think how you think, and feel how you feel.

Experiencing the full significance of a behavior wakes you up psychologically. For some responses this is not enough instantly to break free from the habitual nature of your action. However, the discomfort puts a psychological cog in the wheel of your life. Even without a conscious decision to change the behavior immediately, continual awareness of a harmful behavior often produces change. In any event, the mechanical nature of the response is broken, and your life begins to move into a new level of awareness. Although you may still have the response, it's no longer automatic. You make a conscious decision each time to engage in the particular behavior. Even the most hardened, habitual routine can be broken down, worn down, until it unravels. As your life moves outside the field of automation, you begin to see your true self, and you begin truly to live.

When you become conscious of various aspects of your life, you bring a new vitality to your actions. This makes it easy to eliminate habits because they are only actions that over time have become automatic. Awareness is what dissolves a habit into a simple action.

The complexity of life lies in its automation. Slow it down and you will see just how simple life really is. You will see what you were barely aware of before—the relationship between cause and effect. Action and result. This allows you to understand fully what you could not before: You are in fact in control of your life. You will be able to make new decisions and choices based on what *you want*. This is living. A life that has become automatic has difficulty recognizing the relationship between cause and effect. If you do not feel that you have control over your life, then there is little incentive for taking charge. When you begin to look at aspects of your behavior, your life is slowed. Your life is brought out of the abstract. It's no longer this swirling mass that whips out of control.

Responses are not categorized in any way. Grouping very often leads us to decide where we fall before we have adequate knowledge. The idea here is to break away from generalizing and forming prejudices. It's comforting to put everything into categories, including us, to say, "I am this and I do that." But that's all it is—comforting. Additionally, the degree and quantity of these responses are specific to each person. Some responses will be more significant for you than for others. And as you see yourself in these responses you will naturally think of other automatic behaviors that you were not previously aware of. These one hundred behaviors are designed to allow you to gain a sense of introspection—to see yourself objectively. Once you can do this, you gain the ability to stop automatic behaviors in all areas of your life.

As you see yourself in these responses, think about what effect they have on your life—the harm in them and the motivations behind them. Turn them inside out, spend time with them. Remember, once you see how the trick is done, there is no need for the illusion.

The analysis of each behavior includes three parts:

1. A brief description depicting behaviors, attitudes, and feelings that are consistent with this response mechanism. (The behaviors are also referred to as responses.)

2. An analysis of the response, which includes the reasons it's generated and the root cause(s) for the behavior.

3. Specific exercises and techniques that you can use to break free of the response. Simple awareness of the behavior—a conscious look at what you've been doing to yourself—is often enough to bring about change, or a gradual release. However, some behaviors are more deeply ingrained than others. So if change is not fast coming, this last section offers specific ways to adjust and alter your thinking. No matter how entrenched the behavior is, this constant attention to it should inevitably bring about change. Nevertheless, in time, should you find yourself unable to rid yourself of a few stubborn behaviors, you can do what you've never been able to do before—accept them. That which you cannot change is embraced as your lasting reality. And this acceptance allows you to go on with your life. Even though the behavior is still there, it's no longer automatic, so it's no longer part of a shell. It exists as part of you—and this is okay.

1 WHY DO I ALWAYS STARE AT MYSELF IN THE MIRROR?

I'm not obsessed with my appearance, but I can't walk by a mirror without giving a quick glance. I find myself staring at my reflection for extended periods, often feeling dissatisfied with what I see. I have trouble connecting the image to myself; it's as if it's not me I see in the reflection.

THE MOTIVES FOR THIS BEHAVIOR can be deceiving and are commonly misunderstood. It's often not just a case of simple vanity. You seek your own reflection because that is your only source of psychological nourishment. Your looks fuel your ego. You don't feel like there's much, if any, worth within, so you seek the comfort of a surface worth. It's this surface worth that you see as the source of gaining the respect and admiration of others. You may also believe that the better looking you are, the more valuable you are as a person. Therefore your only asset has an exaggerated sense of importance.

A low self-image often translates into a sense of diminished physical presence. Feeling a lack of substance, you look to your reflection to reassure yourself that you do in fact exist. There's an emptiness inside that makes you feel invisible. You look in the mirror but are unable to connect the image that you see as your own. This is why when looking at a photograph of yourself you often proclaim, "This picture doesn't look a thing like me."

This may lead to difficulty in interpreting your own emotions, to looking to your reflection as a gauge for your feelings. When you're in a good mood, you will look into the mirror to see your own smile, to make sure that you are in fact in a good mood. This comes from a need for external verification of your feelings.

Make a list of the ten things you like most about yourself. Chances are that this will be very uncomfortable for you at first, as most people are not in the habit of doing this. That's what makes this activity so rewarding. Remember, the more challenging it is for you, the more you need it!

Be sure to focus on *internal* qualities that set you apart, things that wouldn't necessarily be reflected in a mirror. Examples are, "I have a fiendishly clever imagination," "At work, I do a good job of identifying tasks and setting deadlines," "My friends tell me I give great parties," "I really helped my neighbor out the other day," and "When I jog, I run a little farther each time." Take as long as you need to come up with ten things, and no matter how "insignificant" they may seem, *do not condemn or belittle anything.* Make the list as well rounded as possible so that a full picture emerges of all the ways you are special.

Now that you have your list, tape it to your bathroom mirror so that every time you glance at the mirror, you read the list. This exercise allows you to remind yourself of your true worth—at the times you feel most vulnerable.

Every month or so, update the list. Keep the things you like the best on it, but make an effort to come up with some new things as well. Believe me, this gets easier each time you do it. And it constantly keeps "in your face" the knowledge that who you are is a moving, breathing, living, growing human being.

2 **Get comfortable receiving acknowledgment.** If you depend on a mirror as your only source of psychological validation, this means you've become uncomfortable receiving acknowledgment, praise, and positive words. Break through this by learning simply to **accept praise at face value,** resisting the urge to second-guess or nullify it.

The next time you receive a compliment—"You did a great job generating those charts for the meeting"—simply respond with, "Thank you very much" instead of, "Thanks, but it was nothing: If I'd had more time I could have done a *really* good job!" Don't make people feel uncomfortable for acknowledging you; allow them the pleasure of paying you a compliment.

If the entire process—both receiving and giving acknowledgment—seems uncomfortable to you, then you know what you need to do: **Start acknowledging other people for their efforts, as well.** Give not just to get, but to experience for yourself the pleasure of giving. Once you know how great it feels, you'll be less likely to deflect it when it's your turn to receive.

And if this whole idea seems particularly distasteful, **ask friends or acquaintances to tell you one or two things they like most about you.** (If it is embarrassing, just tell them you have to do it as an assignment for a class or project you're working on.) Not only does this create a situation in which you receive acknowledgment, but it also gives you raw material for your list of likable qualities!

3 **Learn to trust your own feelings.** If you've spent a lifetime learning to deny and sit on your emotions, then you have a lot of unlearning to do. What a liberating experience this can be—almost like shattering the glass in a mirror! (Although I'm not recommending that.)

Remember when you were a kid, and you were playing with

your hot new race car with the red and black stripes? How did you feel when the big kid down the block came along and took it away? Without a doubt, you were very clear about how you felt! As we grow older, we learn that hitting Johnny isn't nice, which of course is true. But unfortunately we also get the message that "bad" emotions aren't nice, either, and so we have to learn to pretend they aren't there—and feel guilty when we have them anyway.

Accepting your feelings means accepting all of them, good and bad. **Whenever something happens that causes an emotion in you, give yourself permission really to feel it.** If you're watching a sad movie in a theater, let yourself cry—what do you think everyone else is doing, anyway? If you think about something funny at work, go ahead and laugh. If someone cuts you off on the expressway, scream at the top of your lungs (just to yourself, that is) or pound your fists on the dashboard until the feeling passes. *You can liberate your true self only by accepting and confronting what is really going on for you at any given moment, without condemning or judging yourself.* And once you've reclaimed the ability to feel your emotions, then you won't need to check in a mirror to see what you're feeling.

2 WHY DO I FEEL THE NEED TO ARRIVE EARLY?

I arrive to appointments an hour or more early because I'm so concerned that I may be late. I get nervous when I'm stuck in a traffic jam that might make me a few minutes late. I would rather wait twenty minutes for someone than keep him or her waiting just five minutes for me. I'm afraid I'll miss out on something important if I'm not on time.

A COMPULSION TO BE EARLY has different causes depending on the situation. If your destination is to be a source of information, such as a seminar or a meeting, then you're perhaps afraid that you will miss out on something important. You are afraid that things will start without you. Because you need to be self-reliant, you want to have any information you may need so that you are fully prepared for anything that you may face in the future. You don't want to have to depend on anyone for help or information.

If your need to be early is "people oriented," then the cause is something different. Although you tell yourself and others that you're simply considerate of other people's time, a compulsion always to be on time or early is no longer a matter of simple courtesy. There's usually a feeling of inferiority—you feel that you're not valuable and worthy enough to cause any inconvenience to someone else. You have no business keeping anyone waiting for you because you feel that your time is less valuable than other people's time. This feeling of inferiority usually extends to a strong desire not to upset or anger anyone by your behavior. Inconveniencing another is bad enough, but since you need the praise of others to reinforce a faltering self-concept, you are reluctant to be the recipient of any negative criticism. Angering another might cause you to question your own self-worth if you are chastised for your behavior.

Having to rush anywhere makes you very nervous. These feelings are often compounded by a corresponding physical effect—the release of adrenaline. While some people thrive on this sensation, you find it extremely unsettling, as it only adds to your anxiety.

Value your time as much as anyone else's. If your compulsion to be superearly is motivated by an over-awareness of the value of other people's time and an underawareness of the value of your own, this exercise will be especially useful. **Being as objective as you can, appraise what your time is worth in terms of the benefits it brings.** Create this appraisal in whatever form works for you, such as a balance sheet, pie chart, bar graph, or even a simple list. Indicate all the things you do in a typical day, together with the positive results they yield. Focus not just on money-making endeavors but on actions you take that produce other values—perhaps indirectly—as well.

For example, if you spend thirty minutes on weeknights reviewing your child's homework and reading with her, that's a valuable investment that carries lots of psychological benefits. If you spend an hour three times a week at the gym, that's time well spent for your physical and mental well-being. At work, if it usually takes you twenty minutes to organize your materials and record items in your daily planner, give yourself credit for doing what's necessary to be more focused and effective on the job—an indirect contribution to whatever salaried or billable hours you put forth. (On the other hand, if in the process of doing this exercise you find you are typically spending an hour or more on these activities, that's valuable feedback that streamlining is in order. The point is, you'll never know until you take this first step and see what the real situation is.)

As you're doing this exercise, you can either write down dollar amounts associated with specific activities, or general benefits such as "half an hour's worth of relaxation." What matters most is that you put down in black and white all the things you do every day that yield positive outcomes. *You'll find that this is far more than you ever realized.* So cut yourself some slack and remember that your time is at least as valuable as other people's—maybe even more so.

 **Ask for, and accept, help from other people.** Punctuality for seminars and other informational gatherings is admirable; naturally you don't want to miss anything important. But when you arrive far in advance of the scheduled start time, you're no longer in control—you've fallen prey to your own insecurities. If it's easier for you to show up ridiculously early than risk asking someone for help, then you need to become more comfortable with making requests.

Find someone you don't know too well but with whom you might feel comfortable asking for an occasional favor, such as borrowing a book or videotape, or chipping in on a shower gift for someone at the office. (If necessary, explain why you're doing this.) Start asking for and accepting favors, doing whatever is necessary to make it a win-win situation for both of you. Remember, however, that the point is not to create a never-ending cycle of obligations; it is simply to get you used to accepting help from other people. Avoid feeling that you *must* reciprocate for every single thing, or that you have to do a lot more for the other person than he or she does for you.

Also, be as precise in your communication as possible. If you've told the other person why you're doing this and that it will be an ongoing process for a while, find out how that person likes to receive requests for help—as detailed as possible? more general? direct or indirect? Then ask for favors exactly as the person has indicated.

Review your past to see if there was a specific incident that contributed to this exaggerated "early bird" tendency. Did anything tragic ever occur because you or a family member was late for something? Did you consistently get the message throughout childhood that if you couldn't arrive somewhere well before everyone else, you'd be better off not going at all?

Whatever did or didn't happen, **recognize this incident for what it is—the past—so that it can begin to loosen its grip on you.** For example, maybe something horrible really did occur because someone you knew was running late. But does that mean you must always shortchange your schedule, your time, and your life? The next time you find yourself rushing to be the first one to get to a meeting or appointment, stop and ask yourself, "What is the very worst that could happen if I arrived on the dot ... or were even a little late?" Remind yourself that the world does not revolve, or cease to revolve, on your timetable. Also consider the negative consequences of rushing *anywhere*—such as getting a speeding ticket or having an accident.

4 **Deliberately arrive somewhere a few minutes late.** Obviously I'm not recommending this for an occasion such as proposing marriage, making a nationally televised speech, or signing the Middle East peace accords. Instead, choose an occasion in which the only inconvenience will be to yourself. Sit with the feeling of "being late" a while and notice that it hasn't killed you. If and when appropriate, such as at a break, turn to a stranger and ask what happened the first five or ten minutes, or ask to see his or her notes. Most people will be only too happy to oblige, and if the first person you asked isn't willing, simply keep asking until you find someone who is.

5 **If you do arrive somewhere too early, spend the extra time productively.** Make it easy for yourself to do those things you ordinarily wouldn't take the time to do. The world is full of great inventions—books, journals, dictation devices, sketch pads, notebooks, portable cassette players, laptop computers, magazines, catalogs—that can allow us to get more work done. You want to reinforce to yourself that your time is valuable. Arriving early, only to do nothing will not accomplish this. Whenever you've got the time, be productive.

3 WHY DO I FANTASIZE ABOUT SAVING PEOPLE AND COMING TO THE RESCUE?

I run entire scenarios through my head about saving a person lying unconscious in a blazing fire or pushing someone out of the way of a runaway car. I enjoy solving disputes and arguments and settling differences whether they involve me or not.

T HIS RESPONSE IS GENERATED FOR ANY ONE or a combination of the following: (1) You do not consider yourself particularly special or interesting. Doing something extraordinary will make you feel like an extraordinary person. You seek out recognition and appreciation and crave situations where you can help the helpless. (2) You want people to depend on you; it makes you feel powerful and useful. In relationships you seek to dominate others so they will grow dependent on your help. (3) You feel guilty and undeserving for any good fortune received in life. You seek to relieve this guilt by doing something great, which in turn would make you feel more deserving and worthy of good fortune.

When people do not receive the attention they want, they act out in different ways. Babies cry and scream; children make a scene; teenagers rebel. Adults who feel neglected or shortchanged, however, may often retreat to their imagination.

Peter, a thirty-one-year-old security guard, worked in a senior citizens' home on weekends. Every Saturday afternoon, the fire alarm would go off, and Peter, dressed in his official security garb, would go floor to floor assuring the frightened elderly residents that they were safe and that he had everything under control. The fire department would arrive each time only to find no fire and no reason for the alarm. Eventually it was discovered that Peter had indeed been setting off the alarm himself, so that he could be the hero and be respected as a necessary and important person.

1   **Identify your personal heroes, zero in on the traits that make them great, and strengthen those qualities within yourself.** All of us need to feel important, and all of us have personal definitions of what makes a hero. Think of all the people, real and imaginary, who've had a positive influence on you since childhood. Do you think of people like Superman, Martin Luther King Jr., Joan of Arc, Michael Jordan, your grandmother or grandfather? What makes your heroes great in your eyes—super-strength, leadership, courage, exceptional skill, compassion, devotion? Write these qualities down.

Now, which of these characteristics can you cultivate *immediately* without having to be born on the planet Krypton? For example, in order to strengthen your own inherent leadership skills, do you really have to possess X-ray vision and be able to outrace a speeding locomotive? Not likely. Chances are that if this attribute leaps out at you, it's because you already possess it to some degree. Actively search for opportunities to develop and express it, such as taking on leadership roles for project task forces at work or volunteering to coach teenagers at your local youth center. I guarantee that before long, you'll feel on top of the world!

2   **Focus on the heroism in everyday acts.** In a way, this is an extension of the above assignment, for it requires you to develop more penetrating powers of vision—"supervision," if you will—to appreciate the magnificence that surrounds you every day. Inspiration lies around every corner, in unsuspected places—the quiet coworker you pass in the hall every day, who devotes himself to his developmentally disabled son—and in notable places, such as firefighters who put their lives on the line at a moment's notice.

Whenever you become aware that a need exists, consider how you can help fill it. For example, **one of the most heroic things you could possibly do is to be a bone marrow donor.** Just by undergoing a simple process, you can literally provide the gift of life to someone who needs it desperately. To find out how to register as a potential donor with the National Bone Marrow Bank, call 1-800-627-7692.

Certainly the use of lifesaving skills is the most visible evidence of heroism, and for that reason you would be wise to **learn CPR and other such techniques.** But heroism can consist of so many other things as well, such as small acts of kindness done consistently over the years, and you should credit yourself and others whenever you see it happen. **Bring attention to these real-life heroes by acknowledging them to other people,** such as in letters to the editor of your local newspaper. And by focusing more on the contributions *you* make in everyday life, you'll have less of a need to fantasize about nonexistent "superpowers" in order to feel good about yourself. You'll also give less energy to your guilt, realizing that you do indeed provide value to other people and thus deserve the good things you've received in life.

3 **Understand that true heroism does not consist of dominating others.** Don't confuse goodness with godliness. You don't need to do all things and be all things for the people in your life. If you're the one who always "fixes" things or "saves the day" at the last minute, this may excite others' admiration—but at the price of cheating them of what they need to learn in order to grow. Overcome this tendency by reminding yourself that the very highest expression of "taking responsibility" is to live up to your own standards for it and to **hold other people accountable for living up to their own standards as well,** rather than take responsibility away from them. Once you do this, you will be relieved of the need to control or dominate others by performing outrageously superhuman acts.

4 WHY DO I FANTASIZE ABOUT HAVING SPECIAL POWERS LIKE ESP OR TELEPATHY?

I often wonder how great it would be if I could read minds. I think about moving objects with just a thought or healing the sick with a wave of my hand. I explore, at length, the possibilities of being able to walk through walls or having the power to predict the future.

O F COURSE WALKING THROUGH WALLS would be fun; the idea is appealing. However, if you are consumed with the notion of having superhuman powers, something else is probably at work. The explanation is as follows.

You don't feel able to compete on an equal footing with others. You imagine having special abilities that would give you an edge. This response mechanism is generated by feelings of inadequacy. You wish for special powers that would compensate for your real or perceived inadequacies and make you feel more in control of your life and your circumstances.

You may feel powerless in your everyday life, so you enjoy fantasies where you command the respect and attention of others. You don't feel very effective in your life and believe that things happen to you, rather than your being able to make things happen.

In more extreme instances, being part of the crowd compromises your uniqueness. If you are "one of them," then you are not special. This causes you to isolate yourself from others, and you end up retreating to a world of fantasies where you can be and do anything you wish.

1 **Give your goals an overhaul.** When was the last time you did this? I'll wager it's been quite a while, and the fact that you're feeling powerless or inadequate today may have something to do with the expectations you set up, either consciously or unconsciously, way back in the Paleozoic era. But you're not a fossil, so why not bring yourself up to date, starting now? **Take several minutes to review all your goals and objectives, both short- and long-term, for each of the major areas of your life.** Which ones still serve you, and which should go the way of the dinosaurs? Get rid of them—all they've been doing is cluttering up your life and making you feel inadequate.

Now, based on who you are today—your up-to-the-minute desires, interests, skills, experience base, and level of motivation— **come up with new goals to guide you in the coming months and years.** Remember, successful people don't focus on what they *can't* do—*they focus on what they can accomplish.* Helen Keller didn't bemoan the fact that she was deaf, mute, and blind; she worked with what she had and inspired millions in the process. So get clear on exactly what you bring to the table professionally, emotionally, socially, and so on, and bring your goals into alignment with this honest self-assessment. There is considerable satisfaction and joy in most goals and dreams; you need only turn your attention to what you can do—then do it.

2 **Identify situations when you felt powerless in the past and write down how you'd handle them today.** Every time most people "fail" at something, two consequences occur. First they feel the pain of failure; second—and this is by far the more costly—they spend the next several years (or a lifetime) beating themselves up about it and using the failure as a basis for making other decisions. We all went through childhood, so we've all had the experience of not being in control, of having other people make decisions that affected our livelihood. *But how often do you still act like someone who is not in control?*

Review the most painful experiences in your past. What do you know now that could have changed the outcome? What skills or wisdom or perspective have you acquired since then? Which people have you met in the intervening years who could have served as positive role models or offered valuable resources? Whatever your answer, I guarantee you'll realize that *you handled the situation the best way you could, given what you had at the time.* Period. End of story.

Today, maybe you'd handle a particular situation differently from the way you did twenty years ago—or maybe not. But simply by identifying the resources you'd bring to bear if it happened again today, you put yourself back in control. And once you set yourself up to win, you don't need supernatural powers to put yourself on an equal footing with others.

5 WHY DO I NEED TO HAVE THE RADIO OR TV ON WHEN I'M ALONE?

As soon as I get home, the first thing I do is turn on the television or radio. Whether I'm making dinner, taking a shower, reading, talking on the phone, or working, that "noise" has to be on. It doesn't even matter what's on, as long as there's sound or a picture coming out of it.

YOU NEED TO BE DISTRACTED, to be taken away from yourself. You don't want be forced to confront who you are and what your life has become. You're afraid to be alone with your own thoughts, so you seek outside distractions to quiet the noise coming from within. The constant chatter of the mind, the worries, fears, anxieties cannot be turned off, so you attempt to tune out.

To relax, you need to be distracted from your own mind. When there are no outside distractions available, you turn to your imagination to occupy your time and let fantasies fill your day. Your mind needs to be occupied, but the internal chatter makes it difficult for you to focus and concentrate. Therefore, distraction is the only way to get a reprieve. This helps to make you king or queen of the procrastinators. In extreme cases, when your thoughts get the better of you, a nervous breakdown follows. The expression "He's gone out of his mind" is appropriate. A mind that is overwhelmed must shut itself down as its only means of escape.

A behavior consistent with this response would be to dominate conversations where you may talk for twenty minutes before seeking participation from the other person. What you're attempting to do is to provide an outlet for your thoughts, to get them out of your head. In much the same way you feel better when you get something off your chest by telling someone else. You seek to relieve the constant chatter of your mind by letting your thoughts out. A fond saying of yours may be "I can't hear myself think." With a continual flood of worries, fears, and anxieties, it's difficult to think and disseminate your thoughts.

1 **Practice communication skills with people.** Isolation is born of poor communication skills. When you have more of a connection with other people, you have less need to fill in the gaps with electronic TV and radio chatter. Improving your conversational skills is one immediate way of strengthening this need for interpersonal connection.

By its very nature, a conversation is a classic feedback loop: If it goes well, both people feel good and keep the conversation going; if it goes poorly, one or the other person winds it down. Unfortunately, many people who are lacking in only one or two specific conversational skills may have accumulated a lifetime's worth of negative feedback and judge themselves to be socially inept. **Get private coaching, or take a seminar or course in communication skills, or practice them deliberately with someone you trust.**

Soon you'll discover one of the most important principles of effective communication: *Be a good listener.* The conversational feedback loop quickly breaks down if one person monopolizes the conversation; then it's a monologue, not a dialogue. You cannot give your all to the other person if you're spending time while he or she is talking thinking up what you're going to say next. Learn to listen, and you'll instantly improve your interpersonal skills.

2 **Quit procrastinating and focus your energies on a single task until it is complete.** Too many of us allow ourselves to be overwhelmed by all of life's "necessities." Thus we lose valuable opportunities to get things done. There is no substitute for focused, directed effort. How much "dead time" did you spend last week worrying and fretting about all the things you had to do but couldn't get around to? If you added up all the five-, ten-, and fifteen-minute increments of this sort from just a few days, you'd find that you could have devoted one, two, or several hours to something more productive.

Don't get me wrong. I'm not suggesting that you need to be the world's biggest workaholic. But I am suggesting that you owe it to yourself to make your time count for something, whether it relates to work, self-improvement, or personal enrichment. Try losing yourself in the single-minded, joyful pursuit of a hobby or activity you've always wanted to take up, such as painting, stamp collecting, badminton, or handball. Not only do these activities relieve physical stress, but they carry significant mental and emotional benefits as well.

3 **Get the thoughts out of your head.** Write down your worries and concerns and update this list weekly. Just because something is important, it doesn't mean that you have to think about it all of the time. You've gotten into the habit of dwelling on things. This exercise will help to shut down the cycle of mental chatter and clarify your thoughts.

6 WHY DO SOME PEOPLE ANNOY ME SO EASILY?

There are things about some people that I absolutely, positively cannot stand. There are certain traits and habits that drive me up the wall. I cringe whenever I see or have to speak to these people.

O F COURSE THERE ARE SOME TRAITS that almost everybody finds objectionable and undesirable. However, it's often those "little things" that can get on our nerves the most. An exaggerated objection to a particular trait is often triggered by the following.

Generally speaking, the traits that you find so objectionable in others are usually the same traits that you possess and dislike in yourself. If you are undisciplined, you tend to judge harshly those who you think are lazy. Seeing traits in other people that you find undesirable in yourself only serves as a reminder of your own weaknesses. It's this reflection of yourself that you find so objectionable, not necessarily the other person. It's for this reason that the most self-centered person is the first to point out just how self-absorbed someone else is.

You may also harbor contempt for another even without an association to any particular trait. Any weakness in another brings to mind your own faults. In effect, you may dislike someone because you are unable to accept aspects of yourself. You cannot come to terms with your own inadequacies so you disdain *any* weaknesses in others.

In some instances, the trait you find so unredeemable in another isn't even a trait possessed by that person. You have put it there yourself. You are unwilling or unable to examine a certain trait in yourself, at a conscious level, so you project that image of yourself to another, saving yourself from internalizing the characteristic.

An extensive objection to a characteristic in another may come from your past. Anyone who possesses this objectionable trait may cause an automatic association to someone in your past. This generates a dislike for anyone possessing this same trait.

Manage your reaction and use this as a learning opportunity. Remember, "he who angers you conquers you." Why give someone else that much control over how you feel? Rather than use up valuable energy disliking the person, use this as a godsend for a little self-examination. For example, let's say the person strikes you as being extremely arrogant, and at first blush, you tell yourself something like, "There's no way I'd ever be that arrogant!" But there has to be a reason why this trait bothers you so much. Consider the possibility that maybe you do occasionally behave with touches of arrogance and create a behavioral antidote now for future use, even if it's something as simple as a well-timed humorous comment after you've pegged your own arrogance meter: "And obviously, humility is my number-one virtue!" Or if you really come up with zilch, maybe it's because you knew someone arrogant in your past, someone so distasteful that you vowed you'd never be like him or her—and perhaps you've overcompensated in the *other* direction.

At any rate, be grateful that this obnoxious quality is so obvious in the other person, not in you.

 **Accept yourself and others, flaws and all.** No one's perfect. Everyone's doing the best he or she can, believe it or not. Forgive others their character flaws and annoying traits. Use the principle of contrast if you have to; after all, the person you dislike so much isn't exactly Attila the Hun, is he?

And in the process, *learn to forgive yourself.* If you think you've been giving other people the benefit of the doubt all these years, while all the time you've been extremely critical of yourself, guess again—the two cannot coexist. If you judge yourself harshly, you cannot help but judge other people harshly. So the quickest way to forgive and accept others as they are is to *do it with yourself first.*

Find something good about the person who annoys you so much. I don't care who the person is; there must be *something* that's worthy of respect or admiration. The more of a jerk he is, the better it exercises your flexibility. Let's say he's so stubborn that if you put him between a rock and a hard place, it would be no contest—he'd be the only one left standing afterward! So you know he's not exactly the most open-minded person in the world. But if you're looking for someone who's bound and determined to keep a secret, this is what he was born for. In fact, what if we were in a war, and this guy were a POW, and the fate of our nation hung on whether the enemy could make him talk, and they devised this elaborate torture that involved tearing him limb from—well, you can see where I'm going, can't you?

Admire or respect the other person and consider what you can do to cultivate the same quality in yourself. Maybe you don't have to carry it to such extremes, but at least you can appreciate it for what it is and strive to develop it in a more balanced way.

7 WHY AM I SO ABSENTMINDED?

I forget a person's name just minutes after being introduced. I remind myself all day at work to pick up the dry cleaning on the way home, then remember just as I'm pulling into my driveway. If I didn't leave myself little notes, I would forget just about everything. Sometimes, I'm so absentminded I walk into a wall or drive right by my exit on the expressway.

MEMORY IS A HIGHLY STRUCTURED and complex process. Once we rule out any diseases or chemical imbalances that could cause severe memory lapse, we're left with the following: An inability to recall may be indicative of a cluttered mind. If you're preoccupied with something specific or if your mind is just filled with random thoughts and anxieties, then your mind is in actuality *absent*.

Absentmindedness is often a chain reaction that you create. When you consider yourself to be absentminded, you're training yourself to develop this trait. When you have trouble recalling something, your very first thought is, *Oh, I'm so forgetful, I do this all of the time.* This very thought is jockeying for position with what you were trying to think of in the first place. If even before you begin to try to recall something, you already have it in your mind that it's going to be difficult, you will get exactly what you expect. It becomes a self-fulfilling prophecy.

This process is of particular significance because when dealing with your thoughts, expectation is everything. All influences are internal. If you don't think you'll do well on a job interview, for example, although your own thinking will encourage your expectations to unfold as your reality, there are still external factors. When dealing with memory, you are dealing solely with thoughts. The suggestion to yourself that you cannot recall is omnipotent in directing your expectations to become a reality.

Send your brain the message that you'll easily remember what you need to—and back it up. Make the self-fulfilling prophecy factor work in your favor by setting up positive expectations that your memory will work A-OK. Then support these expectations by immediately creating a memory jog or other device.

In today's chaotic and hectic times, we're so overloaded with tasks and deadlines that we've become used to deferring as much as possible. Rather than simply open a letter, read it, take whatever action is required, then throw away the letter (which is what a clutter expert would recommend), 99 percent of us read the letter, fret about what to do, make a note to handle it next week, and add it to a growing pile in our in box, where it may never be looked at again. It's the same type of behavior as driving home, idly thinking, *I should pick up the dry cleaning*, but not backing up the thought with any positive action and thus forgetting about it. We don't take action when it's needed, and this sends the brain a false alarm message. After enough years of this, the brain learns to regard a lot of things as false alarms, despite your best intentions.

Retrain your brain immediately. **Buy a dictation device** (a small notebook works, too, but dictation is best since it's easiest) **and use it as your auditory memo pad.** Capture all the important thoughts and action items that cross your mind during the day, things that wouldn't ordinarily be recorded anywhere else. But don't just let these reminders pile up on the tape: **Listen to them until you do**

them. Teach your brain that from now on, you will follow up on the valuable messages it sends.

2 **Make relaxation an art.** A cluttered, chaotic mind needs to be cleaned out every so often. The other way to put the self-fulfilling prophecy factor to work for you is to learn how instantly to still your mind. Release negative expectations and let peace and composure take their place. The human mind functions best when it's clear and calm, so any techniques you can learn to reinforce this capacity will work wonders in gaining you presence of mind.

In fact, it's ironic, but only by cultivating absence of mind (i.e., stillness, absence of negative clutter) can one truly eliminate absentmindedness (i.e., confusion). **Relaxation means different things to different people, so practice the things that appeal to you, such as meditation, guided imagery, yoga, long-distance running, or other such mental or physical disciplines.** Also try to put more balance in your life by taking the vacation time you need. Plan a retreat, take a sabbatical, go back to school. Experience recreation for what it truly is: re-creation.

8 WHY AM I SO EASILY DISCOURAGED?

I can be so excited about something, and then it takes only one person who thinks it's a bad idea to dissuade me from continuing. I'm so excited about getting started on a new project, and then my momentum slows because I'm not seeing the results I had hoped for. I just don't have the perseverance that other people seem to have. I start many projects yet follow through on only a few.

A DIMINISHED SELF-CONCEPT DICTATES that preservation of your ego is more important than positive expansion of your self-image. You are not able to risk injury to your ego on anything that may not be successful. Your concern is no longer what do you have to gain but what will you lose if you do not succeed. Your focus is on failure instead of success. You are not willing to invest any more of yourself unless you can be assured of a payoff. At the start of a task there's little risk, but as you invest more and more of yourself you are concerned that this is going to be "another one of those," and you quickly look for an out. You tell yourself that another idea you have is much better than the one you're working on. And so the cycle continues as you jump from idea to idea. Your energy comes only in bursts and is never sustained. When self-doubt creeps in, your focus is divided and your energy is drained by doubts and fears.

You become increasingly discouraged because you are not able to focus on the outcome. Your attention is absorbed with obstacles. You no longer see obstacles as barriers to overcome but as hazards to be avoided and warning signs to quit. You will put in effort only where there's a guarantee of success or at least a high degree of certainty that you will succeed—asking for fire before you'll put the wood in the stove.

It's a given that life holds no guarantees, but very often you are reluctant to accept this. It makes you uneasy and anxious to embrace the notion that anything can happen at any time. But refusing to acknowledge the truth doesn't make it go away.

If you have been disappointed in the past (and who of us has not?), you may use this "ladder to nowhere" as a means of escaping commitment. As long as you don't put too much effort into anything, you don't have to concern yourself with the outcome. Ideas that never leave your mind will never bring you sorrow.

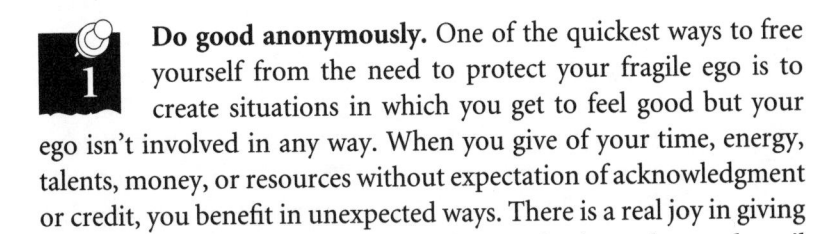 **Do good anonymously.** One of the quickest ways to free yourself from the need to protect your fragile ego is to create situations in which you get to feel good but your ego isn't involved in any way. When you give of your time, energy, talents, money, or resources without expectation of acknowledgment or credit, you benefit in unexpected ways. There is a real joy in giving unconditionally, a feeling you won't completely understand until you do it.

Volunteering offers a host of opportunities to participate in the joy of teamwork, cooperation, taking pride in one's community, helping to avert a crisis, and brightening someone's day. It can be something as simple as collecting litter and recyclables at the park, or as heroic as erecting a sandbag barrier against rising floodwaters amid the fury of a storm. Learn what it's like to give unselfishly and to contribute to a task beyond your ordinary scope.

2 **Remain focused on your outcome while celebrating small wins along the way.** Don't let discouragement get the better of you anymore. Reward yourself for persisting toward the main goal by identifying milestones that deserve recognition. Celebrate them in meaningful ways yet reserve the "all stops out" festivities for the final goal. This is especially useful if you're in the habit of jumping from one half-finished project to another. Considering each milestone as a miniproject in itself gives you the feeling of novelty as you start each new phase, but more important, it also gives you the completion that's necessary to reach your ultimate goal.

3 **Use obstacles to strengthen your resolve, not diminish it.** Consider them the doors that open onto everything you always wanted; all you must do is prove your worth with the right key. Be glad for challenges. Without them, how would we grow?

And for the times when it seems that your obstacle is nothing but a revolving door, **seek inspiration from the examples of legendary achievers** such as Babe Ruth, Thomas Edison, and Abraham Lincoln—never say die individuals who, despite the odds, kept coming back stronger. Once you're aware of the tremendous difficulties ordinary people have overcome through the ages, it will put your own difficulties in perspective and make them seem more surmountable. And, if nothing else, gain encouragement from Shakespeare's words: "Our doubts are traitors, and makes us lose the good we oft might win by fearing to attempt." He might well have added, ". . . and by fearing to finish."

9 WHY DO I TAKE SO LONG TO MAKE SIMPLE DECISIONS?

From what I wear to what I eat, life's little choices seem to be the hardest for me to make. I spend an inordinate amount of time deciding what movie to see, what shoes to buy, or what salad dressing to have. I take five minutes deciding what car to buy, but I can take two weeks deciding on the color.

ALL OF US HAVE BEEN guilty of procrastinating over things we really don't want to deal with. But that is vastly different from being unable to make simple decisions that you want and need to make. This response is generated for one or more reasons. (1) You are simply tired of being wrong and know that if you don't make a decision, then there's no way you can mess up. You are always second-guessing yourself and questioning your judgment. You wait for "just the right time" and for everything to be "just so" before taking any action. (2) You cling to the rationalization that with each passing day you may have more information and greater wisdom with which to decide, therefore making a better decision. The only problem is that most of our knowledge comes from experience, and most of our experience comes from being wrong. (3) Making a decision, even one that you feel is best, often removes any chance to change your mind. This feeling of helplessness adds to the fright of making a decision. You no longer have an *out* should you decide to change your mind. This generates an unconscious feeling that you're giving up control. (4) When you have too many decisions to make at one time, you freeze up and make none because you are paralyzed by the sheer magnitude of what you need to do. Very often, too, there's a sense that things in general are not going well; the thinking is, *It's one thing to have lousy things happen to me, it's another to contribute to the situation by making a wrong decision.*

When a decision must be made and cannot be delayed any longer, you're armed with an army of excuses just in case it turns out that you were wrong. You are also prone to dwell on a decision long after it's been made and well beyond the point anything can be done about it.

1 **Use the coin flip method for minor decisions.** If you take five minutes to make big decisions such as which car to buy but two weeks for smaller decisions such as which color, then obviously your priorities are misplaced. Out of powerlessness or inadequacy, you focus too intently on the little things, and by the time you get to the big things, you feel so helpless and overwhelmed that you make a snap decision.

Uncross your wires and discipline yourself to give major decisions the attention they're due. Resolve that, for the next month, you will make all minor decisions on the basis of a heads-or-tails coin toss and *stick to this method like glue so that you don't even have to think about it—you just do it.* What constitutes a minor decision? I'd suggest anything that requires less than an expenditure of $100,000, or ten years of effort, or the fate of Western civilization as we know it.

After thirty days of this, you'll actually be *eager* to make decisions that are more consequential than which movie to see, and your powers of rational judgment will naturally gravitate toward worthier endeavors.

Deliberately make "wrong" decisions and either live with the consequences or change your mind. What's the worst thing that can happen if you make a decision that turns out not to have been in your best interest? We tend to let the consequences of our decisions assume way too much importance, as if they're engraved in stone for all eternity. *The truth is that the overwhelming majority of decisions can be adjusted or even completely reversed.* Life is not static, and neither are human beings; it's in our very nature to change and evolve. Life doesn't consist of one simple decision; it consists of multiple decisions that take place on an on-going basis, whether we realize it or not.

Use this awareness to put your own circumstances in perspective. After deliberately making a "bad" decision, see if you can live with the consequences, or whether it makes more sense to change your mind. If the latter is indicated, then do whatever it takes to make it turn out as you want. Swallow your pride if you need to, but get used to the fact that changing your mind is *not* a fate worse than death.

Chalk up bad decisions to experience. Timing is everything, but if you wait for it you will have nothing. There's no perfect time. There is no magical, mystical force that lets you know when to take action. A wrong decision is usually better than no decision at all. At least you know where you stand. Thomas Edison is thought to have tried more than ten thousand processes in his attempt to invent the lightbulb. Every time he met with a failure his thinking was that he now knew one more way that it couldn't be done. Be the kind of person who makes things happen. Break through your paralysis by resolving in advance that if your decision does not lead to the results you want, it's valuable input that will help you make better decisions in the future. *Procrastination gains you absolutely nothing—except being another day, week, month, or year older without having taken action.* Let's say you have a great idea for a new business, and you must present your business plan to potential investors. Which will lead to quicker results: pitching them your proposal and risking hearing no several times, or dreading it and putting it off for the next year so you won't have to hear no, while a more enterprising competitor approaches these same people? To me, the answer is obvious. Even if you hear no from every single person, at least you know where you stand, and you're in a position to change your business plan so it can get results from someone else.

10 WHY AM I SO RELUCTANT TO PLAN FOR MY FUTURE?

I spend two months planning a three-day vacation, but I spend almost no time whatsoever planning for the rest of my life. I have a vague idea of what I want to accomplish, but I continually shy away from organizing, planning, and preparing for my future.

W HAT EXACTLY DOES PLANNING YOUR future involve? Simply seeing where you are and then deciding where you want to go. The biggest challenge is actually in the first half of this process, not the second.

You don't want to see where you are; you're afraid to examine your life too closely. Taking an accurate inventory of your life, gaining the perspective of seeing where you've been, what you've done and not done, can be frightening. How will you be able to reconcile and justify wasting so much of your life? Your image will be shattered if it's forced to recognize this discrepancy. You cannot absorb the blame for your actions. Instead you relinquish control over your future in order to justify your past. By continuing to do what you've always done, you never have to question your past judgment. When you are forced to look at your lack of accomplishments, you have a million excuses and plenty of blame to justify your actions or, more appropriately, inactions. And it's this very blame that inhibits you from taking control of your life now. Placing the blame on outside forces shifts not only the responsibility but also the control away from you, in essence, relinquishing control of your future to justify your past.

A contributory influence is the feeling that you don't have much control over your life. There's no point planning because you feel that the direction of your life is not really up to you.

The reluctance to set goals and plan for the future relieves you of the burden to achieve. Clearly, if you don't have a specific destination, then you don't have to worry about not showing up. You may be the type of person who shoots an arrow at the side of a barn and then draws a circle around it after it lands. In this way, you never miss. You can show the world that you succeeded in hitting the bull's-eye. You care little for what you were aiming for; you just need to convince yourself and the world that whatever you hit was your target.

You usually dislike milestones such as birthdays, anniversaries, and reunions. Any marker or indication of time is an unwelcome reminder that your life is passing you by. You prefer to keep life vague—a stream of events and memories.

1 **Reclaim responsibility for and control of your life.** Quit placing blame outside yourself—on your parents, your boss, your lack of upbringing, the lousy hand you were dealt in life—and face the fact that you haven't accomplished what you've wanted so far. *The exact moment you take responsibility for your circumstances you put yourself in the driver's seat. Nothing can move until you take this first step.*

As soon as you lose the illusion that other people are responsible for your misfortune, you claim the power that has always been within your grasp. **Forget the past; it's history.** What are you going to do in the next second, minute, hour, and day? If you fail to plan, then by default you allow the momentum of your past to carry you—and I'll bet the past isn't a place you want to spend any more time than you have to.

If you've been beating yourself up for your failure to achieve, just take heart in the fact that *there's no time like the present to redirect your future.* Maybe you haven't been a musical prodigy like Mozart, composing before the age of five. But maybe you'll beat Grandma Moses, who took up painting in her seventies. Or maybe you'll set an even more inspiring example! Give thanks for the life experiences you've racked up to this point and determine the direction in which you really want your life to go. As long as you realize that you're the only one who is really in control, then you have every reason in the world to plan ahead.

 **Set yourself a deadline.** I remember reading about a man who had been diagnosed with a terminal illness and given six months to live. And live he did. In his last few days he was interviewed, and he said that he had done more in the past months than he had for the first fifty-six years of his life. We need to be reminded that life does indeed have a deadline; we just don't know what it is. So let's get one! We're going to do some calculations to find out how much longer you have to live. If you're a man, start with the number 71; if you're a woman, 76. These are roughly the respective statistical life expectancies. Now subtract your current age. Multiply that number by 365. What you have is the number of days, statistically speaking, of course, that you have left to live. Write this number down, and every morning cross it out and write the new number, which is one day less.

This constant reminder is a wonderful tool to motivate you to take action to live your life, today. You trade each day of your life for what you do in that day. Make it a good trade!

11

WHY DO I PUT OFF THINGS THAT WOULD TAKE ONLY A FEW MINUTES TO DO?

All I have to do is stamp the envelope and mail the letter, move a box that has been in my way for two months, check my voice mail or send a thank-you note that should have been sent last month. But I don't. I'm consistently and constantly putting off these simple little things.

THERE ARE A MULTITUDE OF reasons that cause you to procrastinate on larger tasks, most of which relate to fear. However, if you're putting off small, simple things that would take only a short time to complete, the motivation is vastly different. The name of the game here is attention. Keeping little tasks uncompleted takes your focus away from the things in your life that you don't want to look at *but should.* You leave minor, nonthreatening tasks undone or unattended. In this way, your attention is occupied so you don't think about things less pleasant that really need your attention. You feel more in control because you're focused on tasks that are simple and can be done with little effort.

The impact of this behavior is compounded. The conscious rationale you feed yourself is, "I've got more important things to do to worry about. I can't fuss with these little things." This is how your life gets out of hand and nothing ends up being done. The small things are kept undone to keep you from thinking of the bigger things, and the big things remain undone because your thoughts are occupied with the little things. In the end you sit and watch TV all day because you feel overwhelmed and don't want to do anything.

Very often you use the everyday tasks of life as a substitute for living. Letting the little things pile up gives you the illusion that your life is complicated, productive, busy, and maybe even fulfilled. Your perspective, which is narrowed, relieves you of the burden of looking at the larger picture.

 **Make a list of all the things you have to do that take less than ten minutes to accomplish and do at least two of them a day.** Write this list on paper, or record it in your dictation device (see Number 7)—just get these things out of your head, where they bounce around and take up much more time and attention than they really should, and put them in a form that will lead to action.

Several things are likely to happen as the result of this new discipline. For one, you'll start getting things done at a reliable pace. When you start out, the list is likely to be long. Of course you'll keep adding to it, but as your completion process becomes more automatic, you'll find yourself crossing off items faster than you add them. For another thing, your priorities will become clearer. Not all of the ten-minute jobs are equally important, and perhaps the ones that seem to carry through day in and day out are ones that can simply be dropped off the list forever, no harm done. Is that such a radical concept?

Another benefit of this exercise is that it can teach you the value of making a commitment and sticking to it. Let's say that your list is indeed full of ten-minute jobs, so full, in fact, that you're overwhelmed just looking at it, trying to decide which two to pick for the day. Why agonize any longer? **Close your eyes and let your fingers "do the walking," or tape the list on a wall, throw a dart at it, and see where it lands** (of course I recommend opening your eyes if you choose the second method!). *No matter which two you picked, do them, just so you can cross them off the list.*

2 **Reevaluate your goals and values in life.** If you have to let a bunch of little things pile up to give you the illusion that you lead a productive life, maybe deep down you don't feel that your goals are really worth pursuing. So take the time now to examine what your priorities, goals, and values are. For example, do you profess that health is one of your top values, but you get so busy with day-to-day activities that somehow you never find time to go to the gym? Either you need to act more in alignment with your stated value, or you need to admit that health isn't as important as you pretended and put your energy elsewhere. Once you're honest with yourself, you can stop creating the distraction of a mountain of "undoable" tasks and focus on the goals you really believe in.

Of course, the actions needed to bring a goal to fruition may be numerous indeed. Categorize them according to priority and time required for completion, and tackle them as suggested above.

12 WHY DO I HAVE SUCH DIFFICULTY DISCIPLINING MYSELF?

Whether it's losing weight, starting an exercise program, becoming organized, writing the great American novel, or anything else, it's always the same old story. I know what needs to be done, and I do it for a while, but I don't put in the effort and attention to keep going. I get less and less motivated and soon lose interest. I tell myself that I never really wanted it, or it's really not worth it, and then I give up. "Maybe I'll try again another time" is the phrase that I sell myself, as I have so many times before.

YOU LOOK AROUND AT OTHER people, admiring them for their tenacity and fortitude. "How on earth do they get themselves out of bed every morning to go jogging?" is the question that you continually ponder. You wonder if perhaps you just lack discipline, as if it were an inborn trait. But discipline is not something you're born with; it's an ability that is cultivated. It takes much more than a passing want or desire to bring on the power discipline. Discipline is a matter of training the mind. When the alarm goes off in the morning, and you pull the covers over your head, you train your mind to be lax. When you need to finish an assignment but decide to watch a little TV to unwind, you train your mind to be lax. In the evening when you decide to have a second helping of dessert even though you know it might upset your stomach, you train your mind to be lax. Then, when it comes time for you to follow a regimen, what happens? You offer up a host of explanations as to why it would be best if you just skipped today.

1 **Make discipline a game.** Discipline reflects a conditioned mind. You can't expect yourself suddenly to become disciplined. It's not something that can be turned on and off. Discipline is a mental muscle. It needs to be worked so when you need it, you are strong. Work out a reward/penalty system that motivates you to live up to your commitment, no matter what the behavior is. Enlist the support of a friend or loved one to make sure you live up to it. If hopping out of bed in the morning has been a struggle for you, agree with your husband beforehand that if you do not get out of bed within five minutes of the alarm going off, you will take a *cold* shower that morning. I predict that one "polar freeze" will be all it takes—either you will quickly learn to hop out of bed the moment the buzzer goes off, or you will quickly learn to like freezing cold showers, and it's time to try a different strategy. Maybe your next penalty could be paying $1 into a "pizza jar" every time you fail to get up and treating the entire office to lunch once you've accumulated the price of three extra-large, deep-dish pizzas, anchovies included. (Of course, if you do this frequently enough, maybe you'll become so popular that they won't mind if you show up late!)

Work the other side of the fence, too. Get your mate's commitment that if you rise on time for at least two weeks, the two of you can treat yourselves to a romantic night out. The point is to break out of the same old routine and use the instilling of discipline to add spice to your life.

2 **Don't use failure as an excuse to drop discipline; get right back on track immediately.** Discipline isn't a one-time thing; it consists of all your decisions and actions, big and small, that take place on an ongoing basis. So don't expect yourself to be perfect. Sometimes you will let discipline slide. What matters is what you do in the aftermath: Do you get discouraged and give up, or do you pick up the pieces and continue? *Discipline is the single most important trait for success, so whatever you do, make sure you build it consistently.*

Often discipline is just a matter of ensuring that you have adequate structure in your life. Simplify and prioritize as necessary; avoid the feeling of being overwhelmed by deciding what is the one thing you absolutely need to get done today and focusing your energies on that. If you can accomplish other things today, too, so much the better, but if not, don't beat yourself up. Make your number-one priority the backbone that supports your entire day and act accordingly. Once you have a clear goal in mind, with a minimum of distraction, then discipline is easy.

13 WHY DO I FEEL I'D BE HAPPIER AND MORE PRODUCTIVE WITH MORE STRUCTURE IN MY LIFE?

If I just had a little more direction, I know could be more efficient and productive. I have a problem motivating myself when there's no supervision or structure. When someone tells me what to do and when it needs to be done, I get right to it. But left to my own devices, I put things off or do them poorly.

YOU SAY YOU NEED STRUCTURE. You can do any assignment and accomplish any task if you are told what needs to be done and the perimeters in which to do it. The fact is, it's not the structure itself, *but what goes with structure*, that you really want and need. If there's someone to tell you what to do, then there is someone to say "nice job" when you're done. A task on your own may not have this payoff of praise in the end. You are more interested in, and crave, the pat on the back than any personal sense of accomplishment from completing the task.

You don't believe that you can create and complete a task of quality on your own without input from others. In order for you to be successful, somebody else has to be involved with the process. You don't feel that your own ideas are worthy of pursuit and so any task that you undertake needs supervision from somebody else in order to succeed.

Structure also creates a sense of certainty and continuity. Freedom to choose can lead to regret and confusion. Structure confines your thoughts and actions and eliminates many choices that you might find difficult to make; therefore, there are no regrets or concerns. You do what you're told and let the chips fall where they may. If something goes wrong, you'll be able to shift, or at the very least share, the blame and responsibility.

 **Model your day after someone you admire.** Translate your enthusiasm for the legendary exploits of your favorite hero to the objectives and tasks that fill your day. In this way, your fundamental purpose emerges and gives shape to your activities. For example, imagine you're a knight on a quest. Your objective is pretty straightforward, isn't it? You've got to find and slay that dragon. On the way to the beast's lair, you'll have to prove your worth by overcoming a series of challenges, such as passing safely through the forest of the trolls, crossing the lake of molten lava, and scaling the mountain of no return. Presto, your structure is built in! Now apply it to a real-life quest, such as meeting a project deadline. You've got to gain consensus from your teammates (the forest of the trolls), alpha-and beta-test your prototype (cross the lake of lava), and so on. If dragon slaying isn't your bag, then use any image that gets your blood flowing, such as being a submarine commander or a frontier settler or the world's smartest supersleuth. Once your priorities become clear, and you perceive how the smaller tasks relate to the larger goals, then you get the structure you need.

 **Get clear on your purpose.** Often when you express a need for more structure, what you're really craving is more *meaning*. Somehow along the way you've lost the sense that what you're doing is significant, that it really counts for something. And without that conviction to guide you, naturally you don't have a direction.

So take some time right now to reflect on your most important goals. Why are they so important? What will you get by meeting them? Is the payoff consistent with your top values? If you find that your goals really are meaningful for you, then congratulate yourself and use this awareness to reenergize yourself. If you find that your goals do not give you a sufficient sense of purpose, then you've discovered something equally valuable. **Come up with a new goal or goals that will give you what you really want.** With goals and purpose that are aligned, you can truly move mountains. You will not need to seek validation or discipline from others, because you will know how worthy your own objectives are, and you'll be able to acknowledge yourself on the way to meeting them.

14 WHY DO I KEEP PEOPLE WAITING?

If it's one thing I'm known for, it's always being late. I never seem to be on time for anything. No matter how hard I try, no matter how light the traffic is, and no matter how early I leave, I always end up being late. I even do little tricks like setting my clock ten minutes ahead, but I still wind up being ten minutes late.

CONSTANT LATENESS IS USUALLY A FACTOR of one or a combination of unconscious motivations. You need to feel in control. Keeping others waiting puts you in a position of power. Other people waiting for you is internalized as other people being dependent on you. You desperately need to feel you're in control of something, even if it's just the time the meeting starts or when dinner is served. Arriving early yourself is unconsciously perceived as demeaning, where you are subject to the whims and timeliness of others.

Another factor has to do with respect. If you have little respect for yourself, then you're hardly interested in whether you're thought of as rude and inconsiderate for being late. If you have little respect for whom you're meeting, then you do not care about wasting his or her time.

Arriving late may offer you an "ego-trip," giving you the opportunity to let others know how important you are—and that your time is more valuable than theirs. Constant lateness also may be an unconscious manifestation of an anger or resentment toward whomever you're meeting. Here, you unwittingly inconvenience another because at some level you harbor dislike, envy, or resentment for him or her.

Finally, you may be drawn to the physiological state associated with running late. You thrive on the adrenaline rush that comes with racing against the clock. It's for this reason that you may be a thrill seeker, enjoying such activities as gambling, skydiving, or sports. You may even be known as someone who is reckless, as your need for excitement leads you to drive unsafely or dangerously.

Take responsibility for completing small jobs, do them successfully, and work your way up. Often when we think we've "failed" too much, we suffer diminished expectations of ourselves and are less willing to take on major responsibilities. But we still feel the need to be in control, even if it's of something as minor as when a meeting starts. Attack the root cause of this tendency by putting yourself in control of tasks you know you can complete successfully: washing the car, doing the preliminary phase of a quality-control check, jogging a ten-minute mile, picking out a gift for someone and wrapping it, taking the dog for a rabies shot, making your bed. Then reflect on all the things you do successfully in a day and acknowledge yourself for your competencies.

Gradually assume a wider scope of responsibility in the tasks you take on, such as changing a transmission, planning the departmental budget, participating in a ten-kilometer run, and so on. Enjoy the satisfaction of exerting *productive* control. If at any time the responsibilities seem too big to handle, or cause you to step back for fear of failure, simply break them down into smaller, more manageable components you know you can handle with ease.

2 **Confront your anger toward other people.** Perhaps you constantly feel the frustration and discomfort of suppressing your feelings of anger, or perhaps you're not even aware that these exist. But if you continually keep people waiting, that's a classic passive-aggressive behavior that needs to be addressed.

First, **know that it's okay to feel angry**—even if you don't know exactly whom you're mad at or why you feel that way. Maybe you're angry at some of the people you keep waiting, or maybe they remind you of someone you're mad at, or maybe the two have nothing to do with each other at all. In any case, you need to release your anger before it builds up and either makes you sick or makes you explode. **Find a punching bag to box with, or a tree stump to kick, or some other safe outlet for your anger, and let 'er rip!** Do this as often as you need to. It may feel a little silly at first, but it's well worth it. After all, it's far better to take out your hostilities on an inanimate object than on the people around you.

3 **Respect other people's time as well as your own.** When meetings are held up because someone is late, everyone— including the latecomer—loses, due to a rushed agenda, less productive meeting time, etc. You cannot respect other people without respecting yourself, and vice versa. The two go hand in hand.

Realize how important you are to your teammates and how much your actions affect them. **Come right out and ask them what the impact is whenever you're late.** Once you get clear on the negative effects, you'll realize that you really do make a difference, and you'll be far more motivated to plan your schedule accordingly.

Even with this realization, if it still is difficult for you to arrive at meetings in a timely manner, then **enlist your colleagues' help.** Maybe you can all agree beforehand that for every five minutes of delay you cause, another action item will be added to your list for the week. Use these penalties to modify your behavior to the point where you are working in unison with your team, not at cross-purposes.

15 WHY DO I FEEL ALONE EVEN WHEN I'M AROUND PEOPLE?

I could be sitting with a group of friends, talking, laughing, eating, having a great time. But somehow I feel as though I'm not really there. It's as if I'm detached from my self. While talking I feel like I'm a witness to my own words, as if I were watching myself on a screen. I don't feel like I'm ever fully enjoying myself. It feels like something is missing, and that something feels like me.

A DIMINISHED SELF-WORTH OFTEN TRANSLATES into a sense of diminished physical presence. You feel as if you are a witness to yourself because there's an emptiness inside that leaves you unfulfilled. A lack of purpose in your life makes it difficult for you to identify with other people, because you don't have a fix on who you are and what you stand for. Without a focus, an anchor, you feel transient and shallow.

The converse of this is also true. Someone who feels empowered and confident often has the sensation of being physically larger, commanding more space and attention. Interestingly enough, these people are often judged to be taller than they actually are and characterized as having a "large presence."

Often, there's a feeling of isolation because you feel alone even when you are not. Since you cannot connect to yourself, you may have difficulty relating to others. In conversations, you feel that people don't really listen to you, and you often feel overlooked and unappreciated in your personal and professional relationships. Although you crave attention and praise, you do not feel worthy of them.

You may be characterized as clumsy and uncoordinated. A lack of physical presence means you move uneasily through your world because you lack awareness of yourself. Conversely, someone who is confident and secure often moves briskly and with surety.

1 Change your body language. If you feel invisible, small, or insignificant around other people, chances are that your body language reinforces this. Which person are *you* more likely to be drawn to: someone who stands up straight and tall, speaks clearly, and looks others squarely in the face, or someone who hunches over, mumbles incoherently, and avoids making eye contact? Naturally if you project yourself as if you were the hunchback of Notre-Dame, people will respond to you that way and feel uncomfortable in your presence. This perpetuates a vicious cycle, giving you feedback to reinforce your already low opinion of yourself.

Break out of this cycle immediately simply by changing how you stand, speak, and move around other people. **Practice this by yourself first,** as many times as you need to, until you start to feel more comfortable with your new posture of confidence. Then do it with one or two close friends or family members, then a small group of friends, and gradually increase your new "sphere of influence." You'll find that confidence is like a shady tree in a hot desert—everyone wants to be near you.

2 Build your self-esteem. The underlying cause of habitual loneliness is lack of self-esteem, so work on this problem directly. There are also exercises you can do on your own, such as making an updatable list of the things you like most about yourself and taping it to your mirror (see Number 1). **Start a journal, and at the end of each day, note what you did that you feel proudest of.** After only one month, if you go back and review the pages, I predict you will be amazed at just what a great person you really are.

3 **Improve your conversational skills.** As with self-esteem, there are a number of resources you can use for this, such as communication and self-assertiveness workshops and adult education courses. Obviously this is the type of skill that is best built not by intellectualizing about it but through *daily practice*. Find a friend who is also willing to brush up on his or her conversational and listening skills and commit to helping each other on a regular basis.

4 **Decide on who you are and what kind of person you want to be.** To feel alone is to be without purpose. Without knowledge of who you are, there is nothing to connect with. Do some soul searching. Discover what it is that you want to accomplish with your life. And then begin to move in that direction.

16

WHY DO I RARELY GET A FULL TANK OF GAS AND THEN LET IT RUN ON FUMES BEFORE REFILLING?

At the gas pump I just put in five or ten dollars' worth. I know I'm just going to have to get more gas in a day or two, but I don't fill it up. Driving along I notice the tank is getting pretty low, but I wait until I'm driving on fumes before I go to a gas station.

I F YOU NEVER GET A FULL TANK of gas, assuming there are no monetary concerns, you have, to some degree, an irrational uncertainty about the future. This behavior is a symbolic representation of this very irrational fear. The thinking here is, *What if my car is stolen? What if I wreck it? What if I need to sell it tomorrow?* Of course these things can happen. However, the remoteness of any of these occurring suggests that you are greatly consumed by "what if." You have such a sense of uncertainty that you find it difficult to distinguish between those things that have a high probability of occurring and those things that are unlikely ever to happen. You feel you don't have much control in your life and that anything is possible. This belief creates a great deal of anxiety because your life is perceived as grossly unpredictable.

When you let the car run on fumes, you do so for one of two reasons. Often it's just a case of wanting to create a little excitement, to see how far you can go without filling the tank. However, if you are anxious and look at the gas gauge every five seconds yet pass by open stations without pulling in, then there's a different reason. Here, you view getting gas before reaching your destination as giving in or giving up.

1 **Use the halfway point on your gas gauge as your empty mark.** Whenever the needle hits this point, pull into a gas station and fill up. That's right, *fill up*. By sticking to this practice, you inject more consistency and structure into your days. Instead of obsessing every day whether to pull into a gas station, the decision has already been made up: Fill up whenever you reach the halfway point. This will automatically cut down the number of times per week that you put gas in your car. Calculate the time you are saving. No longer will you have the frustration of rushing off somewhere only to find that your needle is on empty.

An additional tactic to help you keep on track with this new habit is to keep a "gasoline stash" of bills and coins always ready in your glove box, to save you the hassle of searching for bills or misplaced credit cards.

2 **Strengthen your sense of certainty.** Don't let irrational anxiety about possible catastrophes rule your life. Regain control over your own circumstances by doing a quick reality check. Using whatever resources you need, such as a statistical abstract, almanac, probability textbook, or the services of a local librarian, determine the likelihood that various events will occur and use this knowledge to reassure yourself that the odds are *extremely high* that you will still have your car tomorrow.

Of course, if car theft is a concern, there are steps that any prudent person would take, such as **installing a burglar-alarm system or buying some other antitheft device.** If this still doesn't calm your fears, consider the possibility that somewhere deep inside you don't feel *worthy* of owning your car. In that case, you need to **work on your self-esteem** (many techniques for strengthening this are given throughout this book; for example, see Number 15). With a greater degree of confidence and security in yourself, you are able to take better care of your possessions and don't need the artificial excitement of seeing how far you can get on fumes.

17 WHY DO I MISPLACE MY KEYS, PAPERS, AND JUST ABOUT EVERYTHING ELSE?

I'm ready to leave my house but have to play the common game of hide-and-seek with my keys. I finally find them after a brief search. When I return home, do I put them where I will be able to find them tomorrow? Of course not. I never take notice of where I park my car even though I know I'll have to go through the usual ten-minute search. The file that I absolutely cannot lose is the object of another search-and-find mission. My wallet or purse, phone book, coupons, registration, just about everything and anything that I can misplace, I will.

B EING PREOCCUPIED and having a lot on our minds happens to the best of us. However, if you're continually misplacing and losing things of value, there's likely to be another explanation.

By misplacing items, you create miniobstacles to overcome. Once the item in question is found, you feel a sense of satisfaction. Essentially, in a controlled environment you create an artificial challenge that once overcome gives you a sense of accomplishment. This in turn puts you in a better mood. The thrill of this challenge, though, is never consciously examined.

To illustrate this point, let's take an example. Let's say you're driving along in a fair mood. You're not feeling too great, but you're not feeling too badly, either. In the rearview mirror you see flashing red lights. You're pulled over for speeding and go through the usual routine of license, registration, and insurance. Then, much to your surprise, you're let off with only a warning. You pull back onto the highway, and you're in a fantastic mood. *What a bit of good fortune,* you think to yourself. But really, what has happened? What in your life has changed? Absolutely nothing. You're in a great mood because you came out of the situation a winner, a victor. It's in this way that you seek to create these scenarios on your own—situations in which you will emerge as fortunate and victorious.

When setting up these little challenges for yourself, you would not "lose" your heart medication. Nor would you throw your keys into the ocean and expect to look for them later. The goal here is to provide you with a sense of accomplishment. This can happen only if you find whatever is missing without too much of your life being disturbed or disrupted.

In some instances these little challenges are created because unconsciously you *want* to inconvenience yourself. You may harbor guilty feelings and seek to pay yourself back for whatever actual or perceived injustices you may have inflicted on the rest of the world.

If you're a gambler, any gains are enjoyed only because they enable you to gamble longer. You rarely walk away a winner, because that is not what you are playing for. You are looking only to extend the thrill. However, the stakes soon escalate because the thrill needs to be increased as you become used to a level of play.

You may find that this response manifests into other more common behavior. A typical action is refusing to move the serving plate closer to your plate when serving yourself. Or you may not put the coffeepot over your mug when pouring, preferring to pour at a distance. The purpose here is to provide a small challenge and then to feel the sense of accomplishment. Where is the satisfaction in serving yourself if there's no chance the food could be spilled all over the table?

Jump-start your awareness. Often it takes only a simple trick to shake up your routine and force you to notice something that has become automatic. So come up with one or several ways to ensure that your mind registers where you place things. For example, the next time you put down your keys—let's say on the kitchen counter—repeat to yourself ten times, "I see what I'm doing on the counter," and visualize the keys coming alive and eating a pastrami sandwich in that location. Or if you put the keys on your desk, repeat the phrase while visualizing the keys sitting up and operating your calculator in the middle of your in box. The more ludicrous, the better.

Adapt this process for other activities such as parking your car. Better yet, use your dictation device (you *have* gotten one by now, haven't you?): "I'm parked in Section A18" or "My car is twenty yards to the right of the third light pole." This may seem a bit over the edge, but remember, you're trying to overcome a chronic case of absentmindedness, and every little effort made now has a big payoff at the other end. After doing this enough times, you'll find that the process itself becomes automatic, and you'll remember easily where you've put your items.

Designate specific places for your most frequently used items and *never* put them anyplace else. A little organization goes a long way. Once a system is in place, you don't even have to think about it anymore—just do what you're supposed to! You don't go hunting for the fish in the birdcage, do you? Of course not. You always check the same place. So do the same thing for your keys, purse, wallet, and so on. Maybe you can always hang the keys on a special hook by the door leading to the garage (in case of emergencies, keep an extra set in another location). Maybe you can consistently stow your purse on a certain shelf just inside your bedroom closet. Maybe you can always carry your dictation device in your shirt pocket while you're out and about and return it to the top middle drawer of your desk when you're home. Just make sure that you *always* return these items to their designated places when you're done using them. After going to all this trouble, you'd hate to experience that familiar old syndrome: "I put 'em in a special place so I wouldn't lose 'em. Now, where are they?"

 **Take on more worthwhile challenges.** The thrill of creating artificial obstacles can be replaced with something much better: the deep satisfaction of rising to a genuine challenge. *Look outside yourself and seek to help others.* It seems that the world is so full of challenges right now that a person could be easily overwhelmed. But start by focusing on one problem area in particular and identifying one or two simple things you can do to help on a regular basis. For example, find out what literacy programs are being offered in your community and offer your services as a reading volunteer one hour a week. The sense of accomplishment you gain from making a difference for just one other person is indescribable. Don't deprive yourself any longer—find out what it feels like for yourself.

 **Deal with your passive-aggressive tendencies and guilt.** Sometimes, misplacing valuable objects is an unconscious way of punishing ourselves or others. Losing the car keys is a very efficient method of annoying people, kind of like killing two birds with one stone: Not only do you cause anxiety among your family members, who are wondering if the keys will *ever* be located, but you get to make everybody late, too. And if you already feel guilty, and they vent their irritation on you, then it's a triple whammy!

There are many ways of counteracting our guilt and our passive-aggressive tendencies, such as **releasing our anger in safe outlets, improving our communication skills, and building our self-esteem,** and I give many exercises throughout this book based on these principles (for example, Numbers 1, 5, and 14). Go back and review some of these now.

18 WHY AM I SO CLUMSY?

I know where the chair is and I know where my foot is, yet I'm always banging one into the other. I trip over the same wire all the time. I routinely hit my shoulder going out the door. If it can be dropped, I drop it. If it can be tripped over, banged into, or knocked over, I do it.

IS THERE SUCH A THING as being accident-prone? It's highly doubtful that you have a genetic predisposition to clumsiness. Although a medical problem such as an inner ear imbalance can cause some of these behaviors, it's likely that the problem is psychological rather than physical. You may rationalize that you are simply not paying attention or that you have something on your mind, but constant and continuous acts of clumsiness are the result of something much more.

It's often a matter of expectation. If you consider yourself to be uncoordinated and clumsy, then your behavior will tend to be consistent with that belief. You may have been clumsy as a child and still see yourself dropping the ball or falling off your bicycle.

Children, before developing a sense of personal identity, are not able to distinguish and perceive the relationship between themselves and the rest of the world. Awareness of your own individuality is something that you gain over time. You are not born with it. It's possible that your sense of personal identity or individuality has not fully developed. You're unsure of where you end and your world begins. Your lack of coordination may be the result of a lack of awareness of your actual presence, the result of a poorly developed self-image. Conversely, those with a healthy self-concept behave and move more confidently. Coordination is largely a matter of expectation, stemming from this confidence in oneself.

Lack of coordination may be exacerbated by a lack of direction and purpose in your life. *I don't know where I'm going* is the belief that manifests itself into specific physical instances. It's for this reason, too, that you likely have a poor sense of direction.

Additionally, you may be holding onto a lot of anger. Have you ever noticed that when you're in a bad mood you seem particularly prone to such clumsiness? Often unexpressed anger manifests into these acts of self-inconvenience.

1 **Set up a mini obstacle course in your living room.** This exercise challenges and heightens your perceptual awareness, coordination, and sense of balance. Put chairs in the middle of the room and other objects to walk around and step over. Walk through the course slowly the first few times, then pick up speed the fifth or sixth time, walking confidently and briskly. Take five minutes to do this once a day, every day, until you start noticing that you move better both here and in the outside world.

2 **Replace negative expectations with positive ones.** Think back to significant events in your childhood or youth that may have given you the message that you were clumsy or not physically fit. Did it seem that you were always the last one picked for a team when choosing up sides? Did an older brother make fun of you for not being able to run as fast? **Decide that you will no longer allow these negative incidents to hold any power over you.** Think of times when you acted with a higher degree of coordination or physical skill than usual and commit to experiencing them more consistently from now on, noticing and reinforcing them whenever possible.

3 **Take up a new physical activity.** If it was difficult for you to think of any instances where you displayed good coordination or balance, then now is an excellent time to improve your skills. Pick an activity that is not too difficult and that you will enjoy enough to do regularly—walking, bowling, golfing, judo, table tennis, jogging, step classes, bicycling, or a self-defense class. Don't try to set any records; just get used to the feeling of having fun while working your body and gradually getting better over time.

4 **Draw a map of your life's purpose.** Often, your physical sense of direction will dramatically improve in response to clarity about your overall goals. So take the time to create a map or chart that indicates exactly where you are headed. For example, how much money do you want to be making a year from now? Five years from now? By retirement? Are you on track, or do you need to adjust your strategy? What are your investment goals and how well are your investment vehicles performing? What about the area of self-improvement? Do you want to go back to school for an advanced degree, or study law or medicine, or take up a new language? By when do you want to master these subject areas? Continue in this way for everything that is important to you.

Once you see your goals in black and white, you will gain a strong sense of your purpose and direction as well as have the information to help make them come true. And as long as you keep checking in periodically with this "life map," how can you ever lose your way again?

19 WHY DO I THINK ABOUT COMMITTING SUICIDE EVEN THOUGH I HAVE NO INTENTION OF DOING IT?

I really don't feel that depressed, but I wonder what it would be like to jump off the roof of a building, crash my car at one hundred miles per hour into a wall, or take twenty sleeping pills with a bottle of my favorite wine. I contemplate whether pills or drowning would cause less suffering and who might find my body. I think about my funeral, who would be there, and even what everyone would be wearing.

THOUGHTS OF COMMITTING SUICIDE should not be taken lightly. This may be a very serious symptom of depression. Anyone having these feelings should seek professional help as soon as possible.

That said, there are reasons why you may think about suicide without being clinically depressed. First, it's a natural curiosity to wonder about the ultimate act, the end-all. And there are several reasons that either individually or collectively could prompt this response.

It provides a relief to know that if things got so bad that you could no longer bear being alive, there would be a way out. It's somewhat comforting to know that all of your problems would go away, albeit through a permanent solution to a temporary situation.

Another possibility is that you consider suicide as a form of revenge. You get a sense of satisfaction knowing that you'll leave behind people who are grieving and saddened over your death. This feeling comes from thinking that you're not appreciated and loved as much as you should be. Only in your death will you come to be fully appreciated, once they see what life without you is like.

There may also be a power element to this thinking. You're impressed by the sheer magnitude of the experience, disrupting the lives of so many people. This is a power motive that makes you feel important and in control. Here, you are able to accomplish in death what you don't feel you can in life.

1 **Focus on living, not dying.** The best way to eliminate fantasies of suicide is to replace them with positive visualizations of yourself succeeding in life. **Create goals that inspire you and back them up with action plans, time lines for completion, guided imagery, affirmations, and all the other resources that will support you.** Whatever the reason that you indulged in suicide fantasies—idle curiosity or boredom—your mind will now have something much more constructive to preoccupy itself with. Sometimes these thoughts are generated because you're not living the kind of life that you want to. You feel as if you're living a lie—masquerading as someone other than your true self. In this case kill the imposter not the person. In other words, live the life that you want to live, be the kind of person that you want to be.

2 **Turn "death" fantasies around and use them creatively.** In many ancient cultures and traditions, symbols of death also represent change, transformation, and rebirth. Perhaps it's time symbolically to put to rest the aspects of yourself that you no longer need, such as guilt, inadequacy, paranoia, and self-pity. **Create a ritual in which you banish these traits forever and make room for more desirable qualities such as power, confidence, joy, and courage.** Do it yourself or with friends who also want to retire their negative thoughts and behaviors. Pick a special day for doing this, such as New Year's Day, or choose one of your own that holds significance.

If you're still curious about what it would be like to witness your own funeral, read the famous scene on this very topic in Mark Twain's *The Adventures of Tom Sawyer*.

 **Realize how stupid suicide fantasies are.** Suicide is the dumbest possible way of getting revenge. Why is that? Because the people you want to strike back at are the very same folks who won't even remember you a week after you're gone, while the people you want to spare most—the people who love you—are the ones who will have to live with the pain of your suicide for the rest of their lives. *Suicide is just plain dumb.* It has exactly the opposite effect of what you intend.

Besides, practically speaking, there are too many things that could go wrong. What if you drive a car into the side of a building you thought was empty but end up killing innocent people? What if you put a gun in your mouth and pull the trigger but miss? You'll end up a brain-damaged vegetable kept "alive" on a respirator for the next twenty years, continually draining your family's resources, unable to communicate, with absolutely no control over your own functioning.

If you're still unclear on the toll that suicide takes on families, **call your local suicide prevention hot line or mental health counselor** and get a reality check. Or read literature that's available on the subject. I guarantee that it will open your eyes, and suicide fantasies will immediately lose their appeal.

NOTE: If your suicide fantasies are accompanied by more serious symptoms such as feelings of being overwhelmed, helplessness, or depression, please get professional help immediately.

20 WHY DO I COMPLICATE THE SIMPLEST THINGS?

I take what should be a very simple task and complicate it. I come up with elaborate plans and ideas where a simple, straightforward approach would work better. I spend twice as much time preparing to do a task than it actually takes to do it.

M ANY PEOPLE, generally speaking, don't have a great respect for simplicity or, for that matter, the simpler things in life. To some, *simple* connotes boring or dumb. Most of us believe that things have to be complicated and sophisticated in order to be good or effective.

When it comes to our achievements, the harder we work at attaining something, the greater the value we place on our accomplishment. This is vastly different from purposefully complicating your objective.

If you go out of your way to make something more difficult, then you are artificially complicating tasks to get increased satisfaction. When faced with a simple objective, you build your own roadblocks and obstacles.

There's a greater sense of accomplishment in doing something that's more difficult. You feel that your achievements are minimal, so you look to expand your feeling of accomplishment and pride—not in the result but in the effort. You need to be able to say, "Wow, I really worked hard for that." You spend three hours figuring out how to make the cabinet door close without squeaking—not a great accomplishment but certainly a great effort. It's in the effort that you find your sense of accomplishment and pride, not in the magnitude of the task itself. You don't want to take on more challenging tasks because you will have to deal with a host of uncomfortable feelings, whether you succeed or fail. By making a simple task more difficult you can feel challenged and reap the satisfaction of hard work without ever having to put yourself to the test.

You get worried if something is too easy—there must be something wrong or you must not be doing it right. A complication, ironically, makes you feel that you're on the right track.

Although you may be immensely talented, you often dismiss your own creations: "If it's so easy for me to do, how great can it really be?" You end up doing things that are more difficult because you're unable to gain any satisfaction or sense of accomplishment from work that comes easily to you. This is why some of the most talented people toil in activities outside of their area of greatness. Anyone can make simple things complicated. It's the gifted who can make the complicated simple.

1 **Shore up your confidence and self-esteem.** If you've been plagued your whole life by the feeling that your achievements are minimal, examine possible sources for this self-doubt. In your childhood, were you told, "Pride goeth before a fall"? Did teachers or parents place such high expectations on you that you felt that anything less than perfection amounted to failure? Did you come to believe that anyone who had confidence was just plain conceited? Review these incidents or patterns so you can understand their effects, then vow not to let them continue controlling you.

2 **Learn to trust your own instincts and abilities.** Consider the very real possibility that if something is easy for you to do, it's because you have talent in that area. Get perspective on where you stand in life's great continuum: Some things are naturally easy for you to do, while other things are difficult for you yet easy for others. So relax and accept the fact that you can't help but be gifted in at least *some* things.

3 **Turn your behavior on its ear by seeing how little time you can take to complete a task.** Retrain yourself to believe that *minimal*, not great, effort equals great accomplishment. Pretend you're in school again taking the Mount Everest of all tests, and the person who can get through the most questions before time's up is the only survivor. *Now* how do you feel about taking longer than necessary?

Develop pride in the ease with which you accomplish things. You deserve it! Maybe you were born with certain talents that predisposed you toward a certain area, but you consciously had to develop them through the years in order to get them to the point they're at now. Or maybe you started out with absolutely no special advantages in a particular area, but through concentrated effort over the years you've achieved mastery. Whatever the case, be glad you have this competency now and don't assume you'll have to continue slaving away at it the rest of your life. Develop the reverse of the Puritan work ethic: Strive for elegant solutions, those in which minimal effort produces maximum reward. Now *that's* something to be proud of.

4 **Discipline yourself to reserve more time for the tasks that really require it.** Next time you are confronted with the type of minor task that typically has taken you much longer than warranted, set a time limit for completing it and *stick to* it. That way you won't leave yourself any excuses for not handling a bigger task; you'll be done with all the little things leading up to it and still have sufficient time left over. If you're still hesitant to take on the bigger task, then confront your fears honestly. Use any of the fear-busting exercises suggested throughout this book, or call upon resources of your own, but *get help* and stop using "complicated" simple tasks as an excuse.

21 WHY DO I BELIEVE IN FATE AND DESTINY?

I believe firmly that the cards have been laid out for me. I've been dealt my hand, and how my life unfolds has little to do with me and everything to do with destiny. The course of my life is not determined by free will but by a master plan. My fate cannot be altered in any way; I am but a pawn in the universe's master plan. My motto is, "Whatever will be, will be."

WHETHER OR NOT THERE'S A PREORDAINED master plan for all of us is unknown. But that's not the point. You *need* to believe that the cards have already been laid out for you. This response is motivated by several factors: (1) Essentially, you seek assurance that everything is going to be all right. You are seeking a sense of certainty in your life that you don't feel you have but desperately need. If you don't receive good news, then at the very least you can prepare yourself for whatever may be coming. (2) Knowledge of the future offers an added incentive for continuing in your efforts, knowing that the payoff is in the bag if you don't give up. (3) The luxury of putting your faith in the stars provides an excuse for inaction. You don't need to take risks or challenge yourself. If it's your destiny to succeed, then you will succeed; if it's your destiny to fail, then you will fail. It takes the pressure off of making your life all

71

that it can be. In this way, nothing is your fault, and the responsibility is not yours. You don't blame yourself for your actions and inactions because this is the hand that you've been dealt.

Psychic hot lines get calls by the thousands every hour of the day. It seems that the public has an insatiable appetite for knowing the future. Each of us has a choice to make. Either we face each day believing that we make life happen, or we believe that life is something that happens to us and we are victims of circumstance.

Here's a great story that illustrates this thinking. A hurricane blew through a small village causing vast flooding. Only the tops of houses were visible, as it looked like the ocean had emptied into the streets. A rowboat came up alongside a woman who was holding tight to the cross on top of the church. "Let's go, Ma'am," said the man in the boat. But the woman refused to let go. "God would not let me die," she responded. A few minutes later a helicopter dropped a ladder to take her to safety. She refused again. "God would never let me die," she said confidently. A short time passed and a second boat came by. She gripped the cross tight and once again refused to go. The hurricane did not let up. Soon the water rose to meet the woman. It was so fierce, it swept her away and she drowned. She found herself in heaven where God appeared in front of her. "How could you let me die?" she asked. "I put my faith in you." God answered, "I tried to save you my child. I sent you two boats and a helicopter. You let yourself die."

Carry inaction to an extreme. It's in our very nature as biological beings to *make choices* that lead to different results. Even the simplest one-celled animal will respond to a stimulus such as light or heat, instinctively moving toward anything that supports life. But we human beings operate on more than instinct—we also use our powers of rational thinking to make all kinds of choices that aren't necessarily life or death. In a sense, life is our playground.

Experience what it's like not to be able to "run and play." Set aside one day for this exercise (or lack thereof). **Pick a spot, such as your bed or the living room couch, where you will confine**

yourself for *no fewer than five hours, doing absolutely nothing.* That's right, nothing, except the bare minimum needed to function (i.e., breathing). Close your eyes and keep them closed for the duration. Plug your ears. Keep your hands at your sides; if something itches, don't scratch it. You are not allowed to eat anything or even to drink water. If the phone rings, do not answer it. If anyone walks into the room, do not respond. You cannot move for five hours.

This is hard-core, so don't try it unless you're looking for something that works. Perhaps you already think it sounds like a living hell. Or maybe it appeals to you as a restful opportunity to "get away from it all." If you're in the latter category, then you need to do this the most.

2 **Accept responsibility for your choices.** If you're busy blaming the rest of the world for your circumstances, you give away your power to change yourself for the better. Other people have made mistakes, and so have you—so what? *Nobody* is perfect. Making mistakes is how we learn. Have you ever heard the saying, "If it's to be, it's up to me"? Adopt it as your own.

3 **Move outside your comfort zone.** Take up activities you know nothing about, making choices that lead to different consequences, big and small. Or play games that call for strategies in accumulating material, such as chess or military games. Don't approach these exercises from the standpoint of "whatever happens, happens"—**give yourself a vested interest in the outcome.**

22 WHY AM I SO EASILY DISTRACTED?

I have difficulty concentrating and focusing. I keep reading the same sentence over and over again. I often ask people to repeat what they said because I tuned out for a minute. I often lose my train of thought in the middle of a sentence or go off the subject entirely. I become easily bored, even with things that I used to find interesting.

I T'S BEEN SAID THAT THE QUALITY OF OUR LIFE is based essentially on the level of our attention. Our happiness and success depend on our ability to focus our energies. The problem is that you have lost the ability to control your attention. Instead of staying focused on a task, your mind is drawn away by passing thoughts and the constant chatter of the mind.

There are two types of distractions, internal and external, with each one feeding on the other. External distraction is due in part to the generally embraced but damaging notion that the more things you are able to do at once, the more talented and gifted you are. Then when it comes time to focus on one thing, you find yourself bored and easily distracted, so much so that you can't complete even a single task. Your mind has been trained to wander. Internal distractions come from the chatter of the mind; the worries, fears, and anxieties make it difficult to focus your attention. You're not able to clear your mind of this mental static, which makes for increased difficulty absorbing new information.

It can also be said that you lack the ability to put your world into perspective. You have a tendency to perceive all situations as larger than life. Every passing thought takes center stage, consuming your attention. It's likely that you're a very creative person. It's for this reason, though, that your view is so distorted. Everything in your world is big, bright, colorful, and close—including your problems. While others are able to perceive stimuli at varying distances, everything with you is in front and "in your face." It's no wonder you have difficulty paying attention to one thing at a time.

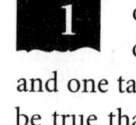 **Carry one task through to completion.** In order to overcome the mistaken idea that the more things you can do, the more talented you are, you need to pick one task— and one task only—and focus all your energies on it. (While it may be true that very gifted people have abilities in a number of areas, this is not the only hallmark of talent, nor is it more important than other indicators of talent.)

The first time you do this exercise, choose something that can be completed in one day or less. I suggest you pick a task such as building a birdhouse, assembling a bookcase, or preparing a five-course meal—something solid that you can look at and feel (or eat) when it's done, giving you a strong sense of satisfaction and completion. To avoid the overload that leads to distraction, simplify the process as much as possible. Break the task into its components, borrowing three very useful terms from the world of filmmaking: preproduction (sketching the birdhouse measurements, gathering the recipes and ingredients), production (sawing the wood and nailing it together, chopping and sautéing), and postproduction (hanging up the birdhouse, serving the courses).

Once you know what it's like to conceive of a task and carry it through to completion, you can move on to bigger projects that require a week or more and may be less physical in nature. Meantime, for inspiration, read the stories of Nobel Prize winners who devoted their *entire lives* to solving one mystery of science or medicine—and what a difference it made for the world!

 **Find something you can be passionate about and become totally absorbed in it.** You can't force your mind to be still. That's like yelling at someone to relax. When your attention is directed outward, when you're fully absorbed in an activity, your mind is naturally quiet. This is why hobbies can be so calming. You don't have to try to relax. Your calm state comes naturally from the intensity of your interest in what you're doing. As your mental energy is drawn where your focus directs it, both internal and external distractions cease. No matter what is happening around you, you don't notice it. In fact, you even lose sense of the passage of time. It is in this state of complete absorption that ideas are created, insights are deduced, and true peace is felt.

Do you have something you are passionate about? If not, you owe it to yourself to find that activity or pursuit that allows you completely to lose yourself, whether it's painting, singing, long-distance running, skydiving, or standing up for the rights of the oppressed.

 **Explore different spiritual and mental disciplines.** There is much to be gained from learning how to alter your state of awareness for a given purpose. Explore different forms of meditation, self-hypnosis, biofeedback therapy, and methodologies associated with some of the world's most enduring religions. With this perspective, you will be much better able to direct your attention and focus your mental energies where you desire.

23

WHY DO I THINK ABOUT ACTING TOTALLY INAPPROPRIATELY IN PUBLIC?

I'm at a social gathering and all I can think about is what would happen if I walked over to someone and called him every ugly name in the book. I think about jumping up on the table and bursting into song. I mull over the consequences of throwing my glass of wine over the balcony or pulling an all-too-obvious toupee off the head of a nearby gentleman.

M ANY PEOPLE HAVE THOUGHTS like these, and they are for the most part fairly harmless. We imagine these scenarios as a mental release. Sometimes the pressures of our lives and the confining social and cultural norms can be restraining. Thoughts of going over the edge and acting thoroughly inappropriately provide a harmless outlet.

Sometimes these thoughts are indicative of something more. Put simply, you do not trust yourself. You question your judgment and have an underlying fear of doing the very thing that you think about doing. This lack of self-trust manifests into a fear that you may lose control of your rational thought processes and act totally inappropriately. You wonder what would happen if you fell down a flight of stairs or jumped out of a two-story window in the event that you "forgot" that it wouldn't be such a good idea.

Part of the creation of these scenarios is planning how you should react after you've done the unthinkable. You run through different options that would offer you the least amount of embarrassment and where you would suffer the least consequence should you lose control of your senses and good judgment.

1   **Do a trust-building exercise with a friend.** You are a good person who knows full well how to behave around others; you wouldn't harm anyone intentionally. You need to bolster your faith in yourself and have your trustworthiness reinforced by someone else. A well-known exercise involves being blindfolded and led around by a partner, then reversing the process. People quickly learn to depend on each other and to communicate more effectively, both verbally and nonverbally. Besides, it's a great way to strengthen your bond with someone who's already a friend. Try it and see.

In general, any process that calls for teammates to cooperate is an excellent way of building trust. You learn not only to place your trust in others but to live up to the trust they place in you as well. **Find a sport** that is enjoyable and nonthreatening yet offers some measure of healthy competition, such as tennis, badminton, bowling, golfing, racquetball, or squash. Or indulge in more solitary pursuits that you can still enjoy with a friend, such as nature hiking, mountain bike riding, snorkeling, and so on.

2   **Find a healthy outlet for releasing unsociable urges.** Everyone has to let off steam now and then. As you may already have realized, physical activity is one of the best ways of doing this. It's much better to release your aggression in a spirited racquetball match, round of kick boxing, or game of tackle football than in ways where someone gets hurt.

24 WHY DO I ENJOY BEING ANGRY?

I find myself getting upset and liking it. When I'm angry, I don't always want to calm down. I hold on to a feeling of anger long after the actual cause of the anger has passed. I feel powerful, more alive, and in control when I'm angry.

PEOPLE GET ANGRY FOR MANY REASONS. Feeling hurt, guilty, insecure, powerless, or betrayed are just a few of the underlying causes of anger. While anger may be a natural and healthy response to a given situation, holding on to that anger is not. It can lead to a host of psychological and physical ailments, not the least of which is depression.

There are several reasons why you hold on to your anger. Any one or a combination of them can be explanations for this response. (1) Anger is a powerful emotion and serves as a mask for other feelings, feelings that you would rather not examine and acknowledge. Thoughts such as inferiority or depression are less likely to surface when you're angry. (2) There may be an emotional void. Anger allows you to feel something, to feel alive. Anger may be the only emotion that you can feel that is manifested and maintained to fill this void. (3) Anger may offer you a sense of identity. You need to have something to believe in, something to stand up for. Anger gives you something to feel and generates a passion for something. (4) You may believe that you need anger and a feeling of being fed up to give you the impetus to take action and make changes in your life. You need to hit rock bottom before you can turn things around. You want to generate enough pain in order to motivate yourself to make a change in your life. (5) It's the only way you feel people will listen to you or respect you. If you don't get angry, others may think that you don't really care enough or are not really serious.

Examine whether your anger masks other feelings. When you get angry, what incidents or situations trigger it? *Identify precisely what you are feeling just before anger kicks in.* Does the anger push feelings of hurt, inadequacy, guilt, or fear out of the way? These are the feelings you haven't been able to face, and they're the reason why you developed anger as a defense mechanism with which to distract yourself.

Anger finds its root in fear. It's impossible to be angry without first being afraid. Investigate the source of your fear. Look at it, and examine it objectively. Awareness is a powerful weapon. **Don't run away from the negative feelings anymore; face them honestly so you can begin to deal with them.** Face the anger as well, knowing it has helped you cope in the past but doesn't serve you any longer. Once you understand the reason for the anger, it loosens its grip on you.

Find excitement in other ways. You may think it's highly impressive to hit rock bottom, then make a dramatic, last-minute save that completely turns the situation around. Think again. After years of letting yourself get fed up, interrupted by occasional explosions in which you finally do something—in other words, undergoing pain that could easily have been avoided—you've taught yourself that life is nothing but a series of life-and-death crises. Do you really want to continue living this way? If you can see that the tires on your auto need air, why not handle it now? Why wait until they blow out in the middle of your three-hundred-mile road trip, go into histrionics, and generally make everyone miserable?

If high-drama excitement is what you really crave, there are much better ways of experiencing it, such as skydiving, hang gliding, rock climbing, race car driving, and speedboat racing. There are any number of thrill sports and adventure excursions that allow you really to test your mettle. Go for it!

3   **Experiment with different expressions of power and broaden your leadership skills.** Passion, strength, and conviction are admirable qualities indeed. Channel the fire and intensity of your anger intelligently so that people *respect* you and don't *fear* you. Harsh, blustery words and behaviors are not the only way to get people to listen—in fact, everyone knows that bullies are cowards at heart. Show that you are in control of your actions and cognizant of their effects. Few things command respect more instantly than quiet, carefully modulated words surrounding an edge of steel.

Identify with strength, passion, and courage, not with anger. Learn the difference between aggressiveness and assertiveness. Avail yourself of leadership books, tape programs, seminars, and courses. Learn what has made world leaders so great and study the qualities of the people around you whom you admire most.

25 WHY DO I DO THE STUPIDEST THINGS?

I'm no dummy. I've got common sense and street smarts, and I've even read a book or two. But sometimes I do the most absolutely stupid things, from buying a car that I never wanted to ordering a meal that I don't even like.

WE ALL DO STUPID THINGS. Those who are confident and secure can readily accept the fact that they've done something that, in retrospect, was not the brightest idea. Those with low esteem are more likely to rationalize away their behavior. So recognizing the fact that you've done something stupid is actually a good thing, insofar as you are able to accept responsibility for your behavior.

Sometimes we're distracted or we make decisions in haste, which can of course lead to bad choices. There's another factor, an actual governing psychological principle behind so-called dumb behavior. It has to do with the ability to make a decision independent of previous decisions. And the higher a person's self-image, the greater the chance that he or she makes decisions independent of previous behavior. If you have a low or negative self-image, then you are compelled to justify your previous actions so you can be "right." You eat food that you don't want because you ordered it. You watch a video that you really don't want to see because you went all the way to the video store in the rain to get it. You continually try to "make things right," justifying old actions with new consistent behavior. In other words, watching the video you traipsed across town to get makes getting the video the smart thing to do, even if you no longer feel like watching it. Your primary concern is being right, even if it means compromising present judgment in order to satisfy and justify past behaviors.

Most people *want* to be right, but you *need* to be right. You stay in losing situations because it's the only way that you can still be right, hoping that things will turn around. You're far less concerned with a problem getting worse, because to you wrong is wrong and failure is failure. You rarely cut your losses, and you throw your proverbial good money after bad time and time again. This is done in the shallow hope that you can turn things around, so that you can be right.

The ultimate example of this behavior is evident in the process of cult recruiting. You may wonder how anyone could ever get sucked into that whole cult thing, where the members give up family, friends, possessions, and in some very sad instances their lives. The higher a person's self-esteem, the less likely is he or she to fall prey to a cult. The person with a positive self-image can admit to himself and to others that he's done something unintelligent. Those who lack a feeling of self-worth cannot afford to question their judgment, worth, or intelligence. The method employed in cult recruitment is slowly to involve the person over a period of time. Each new step of involvement forces the person to justify his or her previous behavior. This is why cults don't just walk up to someone and say, "Hey, do you want to join our cult and give up all of your possessions?"

1 **Learn from mistakes, cut your losses, and move on.** No decision is ever written in stone. The decisions you make are *yours*, and you can change them the moment you realize they are no longer serving your best interests. Let's say you and your spouse go to a movie, and five minutes after it starts you realize that it's the worst piece of trash you've seen in years. But you've spent $14 on tickets, $9 on popcorn, drinks, and candy, and

$3 on parking, not to mention baby-sitting expenses. You're going to get your money's worth even if it kills you!

If you step back from the situation, it's easier to ask yourself some commonsense questions: Just because I wasted my money, should I also waste my time? Are my best interests being served? What about my spouse's? What can I do to cut our losses in this situation? What options are still available? Maybe you and your spouse can ditch the movie but take advantage of the baby-sitter and go out to eat or catch the opening at that art gallery downtown.

Write a list of questions such as those suggested above. Carry this list around in your wallet so you can quickly review it any time it seems you're not getting the results you expected. *Then, if your situation can be improved in any way, even if it's just cutting your losses, act accordingly.* Quit wasting precious time and energy trying to justify a past decision; remind yourself that it makes little sense to compound one error with another one. And be easy on yourself—how could we learn if it weren't for the mistakes we made?

2 **Enhance your self-esteem by recording your successful decisions.** If "being right" and justifying all your decisions has been more important than enjoying yourself, it's a sign that you've been craving acknowledgment. If no one is willing to give it to you, you must take the matter into your own hands. Right now, review all the decisions you've made that turned out the way you wanted or otherwise had positive results. Write them in your journal or in a beautifully bound book with blank pages, or create an audiotape in which you narrate your successes over a background of your favorite music. Then, whenever you feel like beating yourself up, turn instead to this journal or audiotape and be inspired by the mountain of evidence that you are indeed a person worthy of respect.

26 WHY DO I FEEL UNLOVED?

More and more, the world around me seems cold and unfriendly. People, even family and friends, seem distant and detached. There's a void deep within me that always needs to be filled. I look for love wherever I can find it, even if it's in an unhealthy relationship. I would do anything to be loved and to gain the affections of others. At times I feel abandoned by the world and rejected by everyone.

ALTHOUGH YOU DESPERATELY CRAVE to be loved, you barricade yourself in, protecting yourself from rejection, pain, and hurt. Shielding the remains of your self-image is your first priority and necessary for your survival. You won't risk further damaging your self-image, even to gain much-needed love and attention. While you crave to be loved, you cannot risk being rejected. If you don't let others in, then they cannot take part of you with them when they leave. When someone does manage to break through your barricade, you push the person away because you feel undeserving of the very love that you so desperately seek.

Widening the moat around you may be a facet of your own self-absorption. If you are too filled and consumed with your own ambitions, interests, and wants, there's no room for love.

Love, like all emotions, is a reflection, and you cannot receive from others what you do not possess yourself. Those who are filled with greed and hatred feel only greed and hatred from those around them. Without love inside, your thirst can never be quenched by others, no matter how hard you seek.

1 Take care of an animal. Having pets is one of the very best things you can do for your mental and emotional health. In fact, studies have shown that ill or injured people who take on the responsibility of caring for a pet recuperate much more rapidly. Why is this? One reason is that pets offer unconditional love and the joy of giving. They're easy to love, and it makes you feel good to give them your affection. Dogs, especially, seem to want nothing more than to be around you and give you their love. What's more, there's not a whole lot of risk involved with a pet. You don't have to worry that you might accidentally say something to hurt the animal's feelings or feel pressured to be on your best behavior at all times. Animals simply *are*—whether they're dogs, cats, birds, fish, rabbits, lizards, or guinea pigs—asking nothing but to have their most basic needs met and allowing you to love and admire them on your own terms.

When you take care of someone who depends on you, you cannot help but fill up the emotional void. Once you give love, you attract it from other people and are more open to receiving it.

2 Do loving things anonymously. Experience what it's like to give unselfishly, motivated by love or compassion, without being afraid that your generosity will be rejected. Donate books and clothes to a halfway house for battered women. Contribute toward a fund for sending underprivileged children to summer camp. Help support your local library, cultural arts center, or research institute. No one will turn your gifts away.

3 **Love yourself.** It's ironic, but those who love themselves—those who appreciate their own worth and values, not those who worship only themselves to the exclusion of others—are loved by the rest of the world. It's almost like the common belief that banks are willing to lend money only to people who don't need it.

Make yourself an "excellent credit risk" by loving and being good to yourself—*immediately*. Don't wait until you've scaled K2 or created the next big software merger or completed the Iron Man triathlon. Just do it now. If you've been telling yourself for three years that one of these days you really are going to spend a week in that cabin by the lake, do it now. Go to that seminar you've been curious about for months. Take flying lessons. When you taste the zest and exhilaration that life holds, you become irresistible to other people. So don't deny yourself any longer—*do it now!* And don't worry that loving yourself means you have no room for loving others. As the Talmud says, "If I am not for myself, who will be for me? If I am only for myself, what am I?"

27 WHY WOULD I RATHER HELP OTHERS THAN HELP MYSELF?

I sacrifice my own needs for the sake of others. I give up what I want and change my plans to accommodate just about anyone who needs my help. I often come to the aid of my friends even if it means dropping everything I'm doing.

O F COURSE THERE IS such a thing as altruism. But when your own needs are forfeited for the benefit of another, then there may be more to it. You may prefer to look after others because it takes you away from your own problems. It's much easier to give advice to others than it is to examine your own life.

In more extreme circumstances you may devote not just your time but your entire life to other people. You feel that you are not able to accomplish anything great in your own life, so to seek a purpose you resign yourself to serving the good of others. While this behavior may be the same, the motivation is quite different from someone who devotes his or her life to serve humanity. These people help others because they are passionate and feel that it's their purpose in life. You do for others at the expense of yourself.

You surrender your own passions and enjoyment because you do not feel that you are either worthy or capable of carving out a worthwhile and productive life for yourself. Stemming from a feeling of unworthiness and inferiority, your self-worth is based on the opinions of others. You are more concerned with what others think of you than what you think of yourself.

1 **Let other people give to you without feeling that you must give something in return.** If you have been assuming the role of an unsung martyr, this may be the most difficult, uncomfortable thing you have ever done. But do it you must. Ask the people around you for help, favors, or acknowledgment. If they are truly worth having as friends, they will not resent your request; in fact, they will probably be thrilled at the prospect of finally being able to *give* to you (maybe they've been trying unsuccessfully to do this for years). If you dread asking your friends for help, feeling you'll be perceived as selfish, tell yourself that this is a way *you* can help *them*—by allowing them the pleasure of giving to you.

The point of this exercise is not to create additional debts for you to "pay off" but simply for you to see what it's like on the other side of the fence, benefiting from someone else's generosity. Learn that it won't kill you to let someone else take turns cooking dinner or paying bills or servicing the car. Use the extra time this gives you to do something just for yourself, or take some well-deserved rest.

2 **Reconnect with your purpose.** Before doing anything for anybody, ask yourself, "Am I doing it because I like this person or because I want this person to like me?" *Learn to tell the difference between honoring your own desires and merely going along with others' wishes out of a need for approval.* If your motivation in helping someone is to make that person like you or to avoid being perceived unfavorably, then don't do it. You must retrain yourself to do things for your own reasons, not those of others.

What is your passion in life? Why do you do the things you do? *Reclaim your passion now.* **Write down what is important to you**

in life, what your most important goals are, and why they are important to you. What will you get by having them? Get excited about achieving these goals and imagine yourself experiencing them now, in vivid detail that brings them to life.

28 WHY DO I DO FAVORS FOR PEOPLE I DON'T EVEN LIKE?

I agree to drive someone I don't like home from work. I plan to go out with someone I can't even stand. I give money to causes that I don't agree with and spend time on things that I have absolutely no interest in.

W HEN SOMEONE DOES YOU A FAVOR that you are unable to reciprocate, you may become uncomfortable. This is why religious groups offer a flower or some other gift in the airport. They know that most people will feel compelled to give them a small donation. You know you don't *have to*, but you can become uncomfortable even though you did not solicit the gift in the first place.

You may not even be able to accept a well-meaning, good-intentioned gift from a friend without feeling a little uneasy. You're uncomfortable if you cannot repay a favor because you feel undeserving. Doing something in return allows you to justify receiving the initial favor. You often feel that you will be thought of as selfish and rude if a comparable favor or gift is not reciprocated. Other people's opinions mean everything to you. You are quick to help someone, even if you really don't like him or her. Approval from others, whether you like them or not, is essential for your self-esteem. An unkind comment from someone you barely know can ruin your entire day or even your week. A typical behavior for you would be to send a thank-you note for a thank-you note that you received.

 **Practice saying no.** Start by saying no to yourself in a mirror. Pretend that you've just been asked by the membership chair of your professional association to write, produce, and distribute three hundred copies of the annual report by tomorrow. Look straight into the mirror, fix yourself with a steely gaze of complete self-assurance, and calmly say no. Notice that nothing horrible happens when you do this; you don't instantly change from Dr. Jekyll into Mr. Hyde. You've turned down an unreasonable request, yet the world hasn't caved in. Never feel obligated to offer an explanation or excuse. *No* is a complete sentence, and very often will do just fine.

After you feel comfortable doing this, try it with other people. Practice saying no in casual situations first, then do it when the stakes seem higher. Use this process not to create some unfeeling monster who automatically turns down all requests, but simply to learn how to stand up for yourself. It will be invaluable in giving you the ability quickly to determine when you are being taken advantage of. Wouldn't you rather help people who truly deserve it instead of those who are only looking for a free ride?

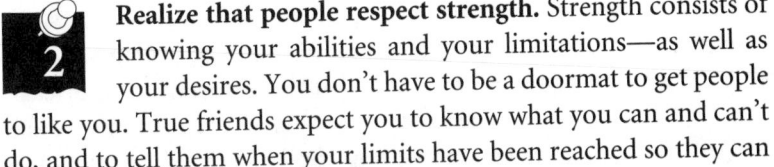 **Realize that people respect strength.** Strength consists of knowing your abilities and your limitations—as well as your desires. You don't have to be a doormat to get people to like you. True friends expect you to know what you can and can't do, and to tell them when your limits have been reached so they can help you if necessary. When you need to deny a request, don't apologize profusely or make a thousand excuses. Simply say, "I'm sorry, I'm unable to help you; maybe another time."

A person who seeks to take advantage of you may *act* like your friend when you cave in to his request, but he doesn't really respect you. He's just using you. If you deny this type of person his request, and he insists on knowing why you can't help him or otherwise tries to lay a guilt trip on you, put him on the defensive. Try one of the following: "Surely someone as likable as you has lots of people you could ask. Why are you so adamant about asking me?" "I have respect for your privacy. Is there a reason why you're not extending the same courtesy to me?" "You know I would help you if I were able to, don't you?"

29 WHY AM I SUCH A CONFORMIST?

I'm in a meeting and I have a great idea, but something inside keeps me from speaking out. Without a moment's notice I can go from outgoing and gregarious to introverted and shy. Sometimes I'm a risk taker, other times I'm cautious; sometimes I lead, other times I follow. My true nature doesn't always come through, as I have a chamelionlike personality, adjusting and adapting to my surroundings, even if it means suppressing my true self. Sometimes I feel that I don't even know who I am anymore.

C ONSTANT AND CONTINUAL CHANGE in your behavior is indicative of a low self-image. This causes you to be easily intimidated. You are afraid people won't like you if they really know you. You mask your true self and do anything to keep people from discovering *the real you.*

Because you have a strong need to be praised and appreciated, you alter your behavior to maximize your potential for flattery and accolades. Still, you are careful not to stick out too much; this is not the type of attention you seek. While you prefer to be acknowledged, you shy away from the spotlight. Too much attention causes you to become flustered; you are most comfortable when you blend in with the majority. Those who are confident and comfortable with themselves have the most consistent personality. The basis for one's behavior should not be based on gaining the approval of others. Your insecurity causes you to seek praise and validation from all whom you meet.

1 **Practice argumentation skills and take a stand, verbally and nonverbally.** It may seem scary at first to defend a position that others disagree with, but this is one of the most rewarding skills you can master. No matter how much in sync two people are, they are not going to agree on *every single issue*—if they do, something's wrong. Be glad that we're all different. If we were all the same, what point would there be in getting out of bed? Notice that disagreement is not the same as dislike. Two people can be passionately opposed on one or many issues but still share friendship, respect, admiration, and love. No one holds a monopoly on the truth—not you, not anyone else. You have just as much right to your opinion as the next person.

So start experimenting with ways to express your opinion more effectively. **Join your local Toastmasters International chapter or other group dedicated to public-speaking skills.** In a safe, nonthreatening atmosphere, you can learn debate and presentation skills and receive valuable feedback from supportive fellow members. Or look for opportunities at home, work, and in social situations where you can make a point on someone else's behalf, just as if you were a public defender in a court of law. Or next time you feel squelched in a meeting at work, write down that great idea you didn't have an opportunity to express verbally and submit it to your supervisor or the head of the task force. Become identified with your great ideas, and you'll stand head and shoulders above the crowd.

2 **Take a drama class or join a theater group.** If you've been shying away from the spotlight, maybe that's the very thing you need in order to build confidence in yourself. Sign up for an adult education drama course, or audition for community or readers' theater. Ironically, this offers one of the best ways to find out who you are: In the process of assuming different characters, you gain a deeper understanding of who *you* really are and what you bring to each role.

Incidentally, a useful exercise to do in this context is to **become a teenager again.** The teenage years are when many of us felt the need to rebel or be nonconformists. Maybe you actively rebelled; maybe you didn't. Try to experience what it's like to do things differently from others, or at least differently from authority figures. Use these feelings to strengthen your sense of yourself as an adult.

30 WHY AM I SO HARD ON MYSELF?

I get mad at myself for messing up, though I know I did the best job that I could have. I'm my own worst critic when it comes to my performance, appearance, and behavior. I come down on myself for things I do and for the things I don't do. If I do ninety-nine things perfectly and mess up a little on the hundredth, that's the one I focus on and remember.

Y OU MAY BE DRIVEN BY unrealistic ideals and expectations placed on you by yourself and by others. You almost never live up to these standards and you come down on yourself when you don't meet your own expectations. A gap exists between what you do and what you feel you should be doing. It's in this gap that you constantly fall. It is here where you live. You are never able to appreciate your accomplishments because you're too busy criticizing your efforts. You are unable to see yourself as you really are because you see only what you are not. Your life is a constant battle between expectation and result, a battle that always produces a no-win situation for you.

While high expectations might be seen as an impetus to drive you to succeed, you probably don't do much with your life. After a while you see little point in striving for something that you will never attain. Your accomplishments are few because you are unable to focus on your goal. Instead you are consumed by what did not go exactly as you had planned. You often get bogged down in details and unrealistic ideals of perfection.

Often abstract self-criticism is employed to mask a deeper, specific insecurity and is offered as justification for inaction. A phrase like "I can't do anything right" makes it okay not even to try since you'll just meet with failure anyway. Thinking that your nose is too big can be expanded to the conclusion that nobody else will think you're attractive, so there's no point in trying to meet someone.

Coming down hard on yourself is also employed as a defense mechanism, providing a way of beating others to the proverbial punch. You fear other people coming down on you for your performance, so you become openly hard on yourself. This consequently makes others take a "don't be so hard on yourself" posture.

Every significant battle is first waged within your heart and in your mind. It's there where you win or lose. How your reality unfolds is only an expression of an outcome already decided by you. You need to be on your own side. Life is hard enough without the enemy having outposts in your head.

Free yourself from unrealistic expectations. Go back through your childhood and look for incidents when you received the message, "You're not good enough." Did you come home all excited with a 95 percent on your spelling test, but your parents showed disappointment that it wasn't 100 percent? Were you expected to go out for the varsity football squad, just like your older brother, though you didn't have the same talent or desire for it? Did you promise yourself you'd be a millionaire by age twenty-five, and it still hasn't happened?

Examine what you've gained by carrying around such expectations all these years and beating yourself up with them. Has the net effect been to motivate you or to demotivate you?

2 **Declare your freedom now.** Create your own personal Declaration of Independence stating that you are liberating yourself, now and forevermore, from the tyranny of outdated expectations. Write down each of these old beliefs, together with just how many years it's been contributing to your misery, and draw a big black X on it. Then declare today day one. Celebrate the fact that you can create new goals for yourself and devise new strategies for achieving them. **Add these new goals and strategies to your Declaration of Independence and vow that these are the new ideals you will hold for yourself.** Frame this document and put it in a place of honor where you will see it every day. Check in frequently to see how you're progressing and reward yourself for every milestone you reach along the way.

3 **Every time you start to criticize yourself, instantly change it into praise.** Since you are constantly talking to yourself anyway, use this ability to build yourself up rather than tear yourself down. Next time you think, *Why did I overdress for the party? I feel like such a jerk!* replace it with, *I'm glad I took the trouble to get dressed up, because I like to look nice. It makes me feel good!* This may seem completely alien to you at first, but you'll get *lots and lots of practice.* In fact, once you really get rolling, you'll probably be shocked at how many times a day you've been criticizing yourself. Use every single one of these opportunities to build your self-esteem.

At the end of the day, you can also write down all the things you said, did, or thought that turned out well. Write them on one side of the page. On the other, write anything that didn't turn out exactly as you expected. Compare the two sides of the page. Which has more items?

31 WHY DOES MY BEHAVIOR CHANGE DEPENDING ON THE BEHAVIOR OF OTHERS?

I'm in a seminar and really want to ask a question, but I don't. Soon other people start asking questions, and that's when I ask mine. I look to others for cues on how to behave, and I feel very uncomfortable being the center of attention.

As a society we often look to others for cues on how we should behave. Most of us are followers, not leaders, traveling along the beaten path with comfort and ease, rarely striking out in our own direction. We prefer to let others set the standard and then fall into line, careful not to make waves. Television comedies use laugh tracks for this very reason. Will you think something is funnier if other people are laughing? A lot of people are betting you will.

This response is present in many other aspects of your life. When you allow your behavior to be influenced by the behavior of others, you sacrifice your own desires and needs to be accepted. Independent and confident people are less likely to be swayed by the majority if they feel it's not in their best interest. They know what they want and do not care if they stand alone. But you don't want to stick out or gain attention as an independent thinker. For you, this label is isolating. You would rather be a conformer and *part of the gang*.

It's for this reason that you often second-guess your own judgment based on the behavior of others. On the highway, if you see a lot of traffic going in the opposite direction, you wonder if you are going the wrong way. You are the one who asks everyone else what they are ordering at the restaurant. You want to make sure that you get something that's "okay."

1 **Be first.** The next time you are with a group of people and the opportunity arises to share information about yourself, be the first to volunteer. Don't wait to see what others will say. Act as if this is your last chance in the world to say something, and if you don't use this opportunity, you will never be able to utter another word as long as you live. In a class or seminar or meeting, raise your hand first; at a restaurant, order what you really want instead of waiting for the other people in your party. A month from now, who's going to remember or care what you ordered?

2 **Get used to hearing the sound of your own voice.** Many people react negatively the first time they hear themselves on audiotape. Don't let this deter you. Get a tape recorder or dictation device and start using it in a variety of contexts. For instance, if you feel that your phone skills could use a little brushing up, record your side of a conversation, then play it back immediately. I guarantee it will provide excellent feedback you can use right now ("I didn't know I said 'uh' so much!"). In fact, it can be one of your handiest, most trusted aids—and it will never lie to you.

3 **Find pleasure in a solitary pursuit.** Spend time by yourself, just being, or doing something so enjoyable that you lose track of time. For some people, this is accomplished by running; for others it's painting, or gardening, or fishing, or bicycling, or hiking in the mountains. It doesn't matter what the activity is; just use it as an opportunity to reconnect with yourself.

4 **Remember that we all have one life to live.** Keep this in mind the next time you're tempted to follow the beaten path. Emerson put it best when he wrote, "Be not too timid with your actions; all of life is an experiment." Can you remember the not-so-distant past, when you were nervous and apprehensive about final exams, blind dates, dental appointments, and job interviews? After all that tension and sweat, what happened? The day came and went, just like all the others. You survived and went on to live another day. So the next time you find yourself reluctant to be your own person, remember that *now, too, will soon be only a memory*. What kind of memory would you like it to be?

There's a great story of a rabbi who was protesting for the sake of a cause he believed in fervently. A friend of his asked, "What do you think you're doing? You can't change the world." "That may be so," replied the rabbi, "but the world cannot change me." Be your own person.

32

WHY AM I SO COMPETITIVE?

Everything in life is a competition to me, and I have to win at everything I do. I see most things in life as black and white; either I'm successful or I'm not. I take great pride in winning, but I am a very bad loser.

H AVING A HEALTHY SPIRIT of competition is not a bad thing at all. Wanting to do your best, though, is very different from needing to win. You have a need to prove something to others and to yourself. You do whatever it takes to win because you are in dire need of approval. You question your own worth and need the praise of others to reinforce a faltering self-concept.

You believe that you have to do something great to *be* someone great. You identify yourself with your accomplishments and your failures. Simply, if you win a tennis match, then you feel like a winner. If you lose, then you are a loser. With each encounter your self-image either grows or decays.

You typically have a need to be right all of the time. Rarely, if ever, do you admit defeat, even when it's clear that you are in the wrong. You can't risk questioning your own judgment and opinions, and you defend your point even if you no longer believe it. You may become even more passionate in defending your views when you have doubts about your own position. This is an unconscious attempt to convince yourself right along with others.

You feel you have little in the way of accomplishments for the world to judge you by. In coming up short, you let the world know the only way you can how great you are. Along with specific competitions, you are quick to impart your knowledge, experience, and wisdom. You are fast to give advice and are easily upset if it's not taken as the gospel. Your self-esteem lies in the value others place on your knowledge, and rejection of your ideas is seen as a rejection of you. This is why the elderly often enjoy sharing their wisdom and knowledge of their years. For some it's all they have accumulated; it is, for them, the only way to show the world they are somebody, if not somebody special.

 Get involved in activities that call for teamwork. Joining with others toward a common goal is a wonderfully tonic experience. Participate in activities that are both competitive and noncompetitive so that you feel the full spectrum of what it means to *cooperate*. Many sports are based on teamwork. In order to win, members must focus on the good of the team as well as do their individual best. Let's say you're playing hockey. You have control of the puck, and from a distance you see a shot toward your opponent's goal open up. But it's a long shot. If you pass it toward your teammate who's in a better position, your team's chances of scoring are much better.

Of course, there are a multitude of noncompetitive activities that also build your cooperative skills. What about clubs or committees at work, at school, or in other arenas? How about donating your efforts toward a community cleanup campaign, where no one receives individual glory but all get the satisfaction and pride of knowing they've helped to beautify their neighborhood? How about volunteering to build and paint backdrop scenery for a theater production at a local high school? The opportunities are limitless, and the need is great.

2 **Step outside your realm of expertise.** Confidence and self-worth are two different things. Confidence relates to your perceived level of ability within specific instances. Self-worth is the value you place on yourself as a human being. Just because you're not great at something, it doesn't make *you* any less worthy or any less great. Everyone has something he or she is good at, but problems arise when you start to identify yourself solely with your achievements. *You are so much more than your accomplishments!*

Today, find an endeavor you know nothing, or next to nothing, about. Make up your mind to pursue it with passion, *regardless of how well you perform.* **Make learning, not perfection, your objective.** As soon as you feel yourself start to gain competence in one area of the activity, move on to another skill that still needs a lot of work, so that you're in a constant learning curve. For example, if you take up tennis, you could concentrate on your serve, then move on to your stance or to your backhand. If you take up the piano, you could concentrate on sight-reading, then on rhythm, then on phrasing.

If you need to, set up a reward/penalty system to enforce the idea that the point of this exercise is to learn. Set up a chart identifying different areas of competency so you can track your progress. Reward yourself at different milestones. But you must be ruthlessly honest with yourself. Any time you start to become preoccupied with perfection, stop!

33 WHY DO I FEEL THE NEED TO CONTROL OTHERS?

Although I'm not positive about the directions, I insist on saying where to go. It's important for me to make others see my way of thinking and for them to adopt my point of view. I usually know what's best for others, and it really annoys me when they do not take my advice.

YOU CONFUSE BEING IN CONTROL with being respected. You feel that if people don't listen to your ideas and thoughts, then they don't respect you as a person. You are bothered by unconscious feelings of inadequacy. These feelings manifest themselves in personae of dominance and control. You attempt to compensate for feelings of helplessness in your own life by controlling the lives of others. Because you need to be in control, you put others down to feel psychologically superior. You utter phrases such as, "You can't do anything right," "How often have I told you not to do it that way?" "Never mind, I'll do it myself."

You may be what can best be called a *control freak*. Often you are a successful, affluent individual who, unlike your unsuccessful counterpart (as outlined in the above paragraph), is very much in control of your life. However, there is an underlying need to remain in a position of power in all situations. Although successful, you still harbor feelings of inadequacy.

1 **Create a "self-esteem" audiotape.** The need to control others becomes much less urgent once you eliminate your own feelings of inadequacy and helplessness. **Review your past and identify the persons whose approval was most important to you.** Are you still craving words of acknowledgment from your parents, teachers, or other authority figures? What about your current circumstances—do you need to hear praise and validation from your supervisor, coworkers, or others? Exactly what kinds of acknowledgment do you want to hear?

Write a script in which all of these important people tell you exactly what you want to hear: how intelligent you are, what inexhaustible talent you have, how much they admire what you can do, and so on. Then commit it to a tape—thirty minutes is about right—that you listen to at least once a day. Put as much emotion and conviction into the words as you can. Make copies of the tape so that you have one at work, one in the car, and one at home. Listen to it whenever your mental or physical energy starts to sag. It will do wonders to boost your self-esteem and reduce your need to control others.

2 **Build your leadership and nurturing skills.** Leadership is not about dominance and control. It is much more about *taking care of people*: being sensitive to their needs and inspiring them to act in their own best interest and/or for the good of the group. Effective teachers and parents know that children learn best not by being held down or force-fed, but by being given the opportunity to make important decisions and experience the consequences for themselves (within the limits of safety, of course).

If this interpretation of control is foreign to you, **read biographies of inspiring leaders.** You will find that all of them were masters at tempering strength with compassion. *Without an understanding of the human dimension, you cannot control yourself or others.*

If there are no children or teenagers in your life, find or borrow some—**spend one day a month with your niece or nephew, or volunteer a few hours as a teacher's aide in a preschool or daycare center.** Not only will this open your eyes, it will allow you to redirect your controlling tendency toward a much worthier goal: true leadership.

34 WHY DO I SECRETLY HOPE OTHER PEOPLE WILL FAIL?

She's a great friend of mine, but I get a sense of satisfaction when I find out that her boyfriend just dumped her. I feel a little guilty for thinking this way, but I can't help myself. I like hearing about millionaires who lose their money and about relationships that didn't work out.

W E ALL GET A LITTLE jealous or envious from time to time, but you take great comfort in the failures of others. Although you usually don't do anything to cause distress to another person, you do get pleasure when misfortune strikes.

The misfortune of others makes you feel better about your own life. You see yourself competing with everyone else because you measure your own success in relation to others. A failure for someone else translates into a success for you.

Whenever you want to feel good about where you are in life, you look at others who are worse off. You don't have to work so hard to become successful as long as you're better off than those around you. You would rather be a big fish in a small pond than a small fish in a big pond. Therefore, you seek to surround yourself with people who are worse off to serve as constant reminders of just how great you're doing.

You see the world as one big contest, where everyone is competing against everybody else. At some level you feel that there is a set amount of good and bad fortune out there. You believe that there's no way that everyone can have everything; the law of averages dictates that there's only so much good fortune to go around. When other people fail, you feel there's a better chance for you to succeed. When misfortune strikes someone else, you sigh an unconscious sigh of relief that you were not the one who was sacrificed to the law of averages.

 **Find goals that excite you and pursue them with passion.** Jealousy of other people's success is a sure sign that you feel unfulfilled in your own life. Seeing them enjoy the fruits of their labors is a painful reminder that *you* do not have what you want nor have you been actively seeking it.

What do you do for a living? Does your job or career give you the fulfillment you desire? Do you have the chance to grow, personally and professionally? Do you get to make a positive difference for other people? What activities fill most of your waking hours? **Answer these questions now. Then, with the mind-set of knowing that** *your success is automatically guaranteed,* **write down what you most want to do with your life.** What career gives you the biggest sense of purpose? Which kinds of people do you want to surround yourself with? Where do you want to be living? *Dream as big as you can and be as specific as you want.*

Translate your vision and goals into a form you can "check in with" every day—audiotape, picture, chart, list, poster—and make it graphic and vivid. This makes it possible for you to be fulfilled *the very moment you set out toward your new goals,* gaining joy not only from reaching the destination but from the process of getting there as well.

2 **Realize that life is not a zero-sum game.** Contrary to what you may have been told when growing up, there is not a limited supply of resources out there. When one person wins, everyone wins. Every victory one person makes is a breakthrough for all. Whenever an Olympic swimmer sets a new world record, it inspires others to call on the best within them and go *beyond* that achievement to set new records of human performance. Whenever a geneticist unlocks new secrets of the DNA molecule, it adds to our knowledge base and enables us to better the human condition.

In the words of the great seventeenth-century English poet John Donne, "No man is an island, entire of itself; every man is a piece of the continent . . . any man's death diminishes me, because I am involved in mankind; and therefore never send to know for whom the bell tolls; it tolls for thee."

35 WHY DO I OBSESS OVER THE LITTLEST, STUPIDEST THINGS?

It can be anything. A button falls off my shirt; my drink spills on the chair; someone accidentally cuts me off on the road. I become so enraged, it's as if it were a major catastrophe. I'm known for having a short fuse and a bad temper. I fly off the handle over just about anything. I become enraged, hostile, and aggressive toward anyone for almost any reason. I am easily frustrated with people who do not see my point right away.

Y OU MAY HAVE NOTHING in your life to absorb your energy. Without something that consumes your passion and energy you have no anchor, nothing that grounds you and offers perspective about what is really important in your life. Focus and purpose are what give one perspective, and you lack these.

Without a focus, you lose proper perspective, and the little things soak up ever more of your attention. The person who has a full life doesn't fret the little stuff. This is why people say that a near-death experience changes their entire life. It puts things into perspective. After having almost died, somehow the scratch in the dining-room floor doesn't seem as important. Perspective determines exactly how we see our world. Without something to move toward, something to focus your attention on, you lose all perspective. Any little thing that comes up is no longer part of your life. It *is* your life.

When you obsess over the little things, you leave little time and attention for going after the big things. Fretting the small stuff allows you to be occupied without facing any of the real challenges in life.

You become increasingly frustrated when little things don't go your way because you are aware that you don't have much going on, and you become frustrated even more because *all you have is the small stuff*. When even minor things go wrong, you feel like nothing is going right. A familiar phrase uttered may be, "Can't I have anything nice in my life?" This frustration is often directed outward. You become short-tempered and frustrated when other people are not "perfect." You find fault and problems in almost any encounter and have absolutely no patience for anything and anyone when you're in your frustration mode.

Because you are not securely anchored psychologically, you are fast to become emotionally paralyzed when you have something on your mind. It's for this reason that you don't handle stress very well. You're not able to focus or work on any task while you have something "hanging over your head." You don't deal with the challenges of everyday life particularly well because every little thing is seen as a big problem. You may be highly prone to hypochondria because every aspect of yourself is magnified. With constant and continuous scrutiny on almost anything, you are sure to find cause for dissatisfaction.

If you've ever found yourself in a relationship that ended abruptly and seemingly without reason, this may be the root. If your partner was floundering, with no real direction and goals, she saw the relationship as an anchor, something permanent to grasp. Once this person became more settled in other areas of life, the stability of the relationship was no longer needed. To you it looks as if your partner's feelings for you changed, when in actuality it's her relationship with herself that changed.

 **Each morning, remind yourself of the things in life that are really important.** There is no quicker way to regain perspective. Are you still alive? Do you live in a free country? Do you have the ability to decide what to do with your own life? Do you have air to breathe? Can you feel the sunshine on your face? *Count your blessings and give thanks for all the gifts you already have.*

Contrast your experience with those of others who had less. Read books or watch movies that will make you realize just how lucky you are. Read Anne Frank's *The Diary of a Young Girl*, the true story of two Jewish families who were forced to hide in a tiny attic *for years* in Nazi-occupied Amsterdam during World War II. Whoever reads this book cannot fail to be moved by the will of the human spirit to survive despite the most appalling conditions.

Create a visual reminder that helps you set priorities. Buy two fishbowls or glass jars, one large and one small. Label the big jar "Little Stuff." On white strips of paper (the same size as what you find in fortune cookies) write all the little things that tend to drive you nuts, such as finding a wet towel on the bed or spilling cereal all over the floor. Put these strips in the big jar. Whenever you react out of proportion to anything else that's small, write that down, too, and stuff it into the jar. Pretty soon you'll have lots of little things collected; in fact, most of what you write down will be "Little Stuff." *These are the things you don't need to worry about.*

Label the little jar "Big Stuff." Be very selective about what you put into this jar; it's best to reserve it for the most important things, such as what career you want to have five years from now or whether you want to have children. Write these things on little strips of gold paper and put them in the "Big Stuff" jar. *These are the things worth focusing on.*

Every couple of months or so, empty the jars. Review what's written on the gold strips: Are they still worth keeping in "Big Stuff"? If not, discard them and replace them with any others that have become important. With the white strips, a "farewell" ritual is in order. Burn them or otherwise get rid of them with a flourish and enjoy freeing yourself from the "Little Stuff." Start the month anew with an empty "Little Stuff" jar and see if it takes longer to fill up this time.

36 WHY DO I FEEL THAT SOMETHING BAD WILL HAPPEN TO ME IF SOMETHING GOOD HAPPENS?

After finding a great parking spot I think, Just wait, I'll bet someone bangs into me here. *I'm not able to accept either unexpected or expected good fortune without a nagging feeling that it's going to "even out" in the end; I fear that I'm going to pay the price later. I'm never able to enjoy completely good fortune because I'm always wondering when the other shoe will drop.*

F EELING THAT GOOD FORTUNE always has a "catch" is a fairly common belief, fostered in part by the fact that many things in life really do have a catch. A friend will do a favor, but only if . . . I am "guaranteed" to win if . . . Ever since we were little we've heard various droplets of wisdom: "You get nothing for nothing," "You get what you pay for," "There are no free lunches." While this thinking is not without its practicality, if you absolutely cannot accept any good fortune whatsoever, then your thinking is not so common.

Whether or not you are comfortable receiving good fortune depends on a simple criterion. If you feel you deserve good fortune, then you are comfortable receiving it. And yes, some people just don't feel deserving of a good parking spot. When unexpected fortune comes your way, there is an anxiety brought on by this feeling of unworth. While it may be difficult to embrace this good fortune, you nonetheless have it. The greater challenge comes with the things in life that you have control over and recognizing how you sabotage your own successes.

Having a low self-image and feeling unworthy of good fortune alter your behavior, so that your performance is consistent with your self-image. In other words, you have an image of yourself and mold your thoughts and behavior around this perception. Let's say you're playing a round of golf and doing well. After nine holes you realize that if you continue at this pace you will play your best game ever. What happens? Suddenly your game begins to turn, and you end up with a score that you feel, albeit unconsciously, you should get. Or more accurately, one that you feel worthy of. Simply, your performance is consistent with your perception of what type of golfer you are. By sabotaging your success you fulfill your personal prophecy and in a warped sense give yourself a sense of security. The outcome is consistent with your thinking. And all is well. Your life is in balance, and there were no surprises for you today.

This is exactly why when you're in a good mood and you feel on top of the world, you do better than when you're feeling down on yourself. You have, at least temporarily, a positive self-image, and your thoughts and actions are consistent with someone who feels that he or she can and should perform well. Consequently, when you are feeling down, your performance reflects the actions produced by someone who does not feel worthy of doing well.

So feeling that something bad will happen if something good happens does ironically become your reality. You are justified in this thinking because you are constantly adjusting your behavior to conform to your expectations. Besides the psychological comfort of consistency, this response is maintained to give you a good feeling when nothing good happens and keeps you from pursuing the better things in life. To you, lack of good fortune means only that you don't have to worry about something bad happening to balance it out.

1 **Create a scenario that allows you to accept good luck.**
The less you welcome good fortune into your life, the less
it will come knocking on your door. To break through
feelings of unworth or superstition, visualize something that takes
you off the hook and leaves you with no responsibility at all except
that of enjoying the unexpected windfall. For example, imagine that
a helpful genie or guardian angel or long-gone ancestor in spirit form
is watching over you, protecting you, and helping you along. If
you've been afraid of enjoying too much good fortune for fear the
evil eye will punish you, let your guardian spirit, not you, deal with
the evil eye. Or consider that when good fortune strikes it's to balance out all the bad luck that has previously come your way, not the
other way around. Or imagine that life is one giant chessboard, and
for some reason you may never know you've been moved into a
square that brings you certain advantages.

Relax, accept your good luck, and give thanks for it. Realizing that
the quickest way to chase away good fortune is to question it, and
the surest way of attracting more is to enjoy it whenever it falls into
your lap.

2 **Replace negative expectations with positive expectations.** Give your mind something better to occupy itself
with than self-sabotage. Remember that good things don't
happen singly; they tend to happen in groups. So the next time
something good happens, get excited—you're on a roll, and you're
likely to receive even more good luck in the immediate future!

Every time something good happens, repeat to yourself at least
ten times, *without exception*, "I'm so grateful for my good fortune.
I'm glad it happened, because I'm worth it, and I deserve even
more!" Then visualize exactly what would happen if things kept
going your way. Would you continue to score subpar on the re-
maining nine holes of golf and indeed have your greatest game ever?
At work, would you get not only the raise you asked for but a pro-
motion and acknowledgment as well? *Dare to dream, and dream big.*

3 **Ask for what you want.** Once a day, ask someone for something. It can be big, medium, or small, but get used to saying what you want. After all, no one's a mind reader; if you don't give people an opportunity, how can they help you? Ask for a lift to work; ask for help writing a report. Don't stick to trivial requests; make sure that you ask for something fairly major at least once a week. Once you're comfortable asking and receiving, you won't be so eager to chase good fortune away.

37 WHY DO I LOOK AT MY WATCH TO SEE IF I'M HUNGRY OR TIRED?

I glance at my watch and realize it's already four o'clock. Since I haven't eaten in five hours, I think to myself that I must be hungry. I don't feel hungry, but I eat anyway because I must be. I wake up in the morning feeling refreshed only to look at the clock that shows that I still have two hours before I have to get up for work. Suddenly I feel tired and go back to bed.

YOU LOOK FOR EXTERNAL VERIFICATION and validation of your feelings because of a lack self-trust. You are unsure of yourself, and you don't put much faith in your intuition or instinct. You no longer trust your judgment, and when unsure about a course of action you seek as much tangible proof as possible before making a decision. Instinct is rarely included in your equation, because if it turns out to be a wrong decision, you need to be able to point to the facts, the proof, to justify your behavior. You need to be able to justify your actions based on proof of external evidence and not on a gut feeling.

You're tired of being wrong and feel you no longer have the ability to make good decisions based on your own judgment. You care for things that are standardized and don't care much for, or understand, the idea of "customization." You prefer other people to set the standard for what is good and proper.

For one weekend or one week, live without watches and clocks. In today's hurry-up world, this is a bigger stretch than you might think. Practically everywhere we look we're confronted with the time: wristwatches, pagers, VCRs, wall clocks at work, microwave ovens, computers. Whenever we pick up messages from voice mail or answering machines, we hear what time of day the call came in.

Take off your wristwatch and put it in a drawer for the weekend. "Zero out" all the clocks in your house, or turn them around to face the wall. You'll be surprised at just how dependent you are on the time to tell you what to do and when to do it.

By living without your wristwatch for a few days, you will learn to rely more on your own feelings of hunger, need for sleep, and so on. If a week or a weekend doesn't do the trick, lengthen the period of time. Eventually you will notice results.

Do activities that don't have "right" or "wrong" choices. If you take decision making much too seriously, you need to learn how much fun it is to trust your judgment and rely on your instincts. Creative pursuits are an excellent way of achieving this end. Do something simply for the fun of doing it, such as molding a piece of clay or painting a picture or writing free verse or inventing a tune on the piano. *Do it until you—and you alone—are satisfied with the results.* You don't have to live up to anybody else's expectations. After all, it's your own creation and no one else's. If your painting lacks realism and perspective, so what? If the ceramic figure you create has two thumbs on each hand, who cares? Just do it the way you want and give yourself room to let your imagination soar.

38

WHY DO I GET A NAGGING FEELING THAT I'M FORGETTING SOMETHING?

I can't put my finger on it, but I can't shake this constant nagging feeling that I'm always forgetting something. It's either something I should have done or something I need to do. I'm usually on top of things, but I still feel as if I've missed something. Whenever I go away on vacation, no matter how many times I check my don't-forget list, I just "know" there's something that I'm forgetting.

THIS BEHAVIOR IS DIFFERENT from the person who is absent-minded in that here there is only the perception that you have forgotten something. This response manifests from an unconscious feeling that you're not doing what you really want to be doing or from the feeling that you are missing out on something in your life. This feeling translates into a conscious sensation that you're forgetting to do something.

If you're an accountant and all the while suppress your desire to be a musician, then that sublimation is manifested into a feeling that you have forgotten to do something specific. Your mind is unable to accept and recognize an unfulfilled aspiration, so it surfaces as an abstract sensation.

Because of these feelings, you often second-guess your decisions and judgment. At the core of this behavior is a feeling of self-doubt. You do not place a great deal of confidence in your judgment and, in essence, distrust your ability to handle yourself. You need to keep checking up on yourself to make sure that whatever actions you do take you do not mess up.

This can create a compulsion because you feel a need to check yourself. You check to see if you turned the stove off even though you're "pretty sure" that you did. You keep going back to the door, the window, the car to "double-check." You drive back ten miles because you're not sure if you closed the garage door.

1 Ask yourself, "What would I do if it were impossible to fail?" This is called "no limits" thinking. You don't need anyone else's permission to dream, just your own. Once you find your dream, decide what steps you can take toward making it a reality. Why waste any more time coming up with reasons not to do something, when all you really need is one reason why you should?

When your life is focused on a driving ambition, you lose the need to obsess on little things like wondering whether you really shut the garage door. Being compelled by an exciting vision replaces self-doubt with certainty. *Get yourself a purpose, and you'll find your energies automatically concentrating themselves to help manifest your desire.*

2 Sharpen your memory skills. If you haven't already started a journal, do so now. Every day, write down the most important activities, thoughts, dreams, and accomplishments you had. It's amazing how many significant moments we have in a day but don't take full advantage of because we never record them and let them sink into our consciousness. Don't let that happen to you—give your life the attention it deserves.

After a year, go back and read what you've written. I predict you'll be pleasantly surprised at the level of insight you displayed. Keep it up and make journaling a lifetime habit. *The more you do it, the better you get at it.*

39 WHY DO I LIVE IN COMPLETE FEAR OF MY LOVED ONES BEING INJURED OR KILLED?

Several times throughout the day I think about what would happen if someone I cared about passed away. If a family member is late returning home, my imagination begins to explore every horrible scenario. I can be in a great mood, then suddenly I start to think, "what if . . ."

C LEARLY THE LOSS OF a family member or close friend can be a traumatic experience. Healthy concerns for your loved ones' well-being is only natural. However, when these fears and worries occupy your thoughts constantly and consistently, to the point that they interfere with your quality of life, it is not only unnatural but very unhealthy.

This type of obsessive worrying may be the result of a general anxiety. However, if it's so pervasive and dominant that it is your main source of anxiety, then there probably is a more specific cause. It's likely that you connect your own self-worth and identity to other people. The death of another means the psychological death of yourself, because your entire reason for living is for the respect, love, and admiration of the people you care about. If the person to whom you've attached your purpose dies then your very reason for living is invalidated. Many successful people often say that their greatest regret is not having their parents alive to see their achievements. If your parents were the source of your purpose, you might not even be able to move toward achievement because your incentive is absent.

You need your accomplishments to be known to the world and, more important, to those you care about. You feel you're running against the clock. You need to gain the respect and pride of all the people in your life before it becomes too late. This anxiety can stifle your passion and pursuits. You live with the greatest uncertainty and may become psychologically frozen.

Your life will no longer be livable, it will no longer have purpose or meaning, if someone dies. You become paralyzed by this fear and often see no point in working toward something if your life can become pointless in a moment. You feel you have something to prove but are faced with a quandary. You're torn between working hard and risking that you won't "finish in time" versus not doing anything but not feeling let down by *coming so close*. This lack of control and uncertainty builds its own web of worries and concerns as your mind races to comfort itself. You feel hurried and under pressure because you have this covert deadline, but you rarely associate its source to this fear.

1 **Tell the important people in your life how much they mean to you.** Don't wait another minute; pick up the phone or write a letter and let them know that you love them, admire them, or care for them. If you wait for a "good enough" reason to do so, that reason may never come. So do it *now*.

Call your parents or visit them. Write them a poem or sing them a song. Send a letter to your sixth-grade teacher or Little League coach, letting him or her know what a big difference he or she made in your life. Tape a message for your children or grandchildren telling them just how special they are.

When we pass up opportunities to add joy to someone's life, we cheat not only the other person but also ourselves. Don't deny yourself any longer.

 **Strengthen your own identity by reconnecting with your personal vision.** While it's a great feeling to have the respect and admiration of those we love, your pursuits in life should give you pride in yourself. Live the kind of life that *you* want to live; pursue the goals and dreams that fulfill you as a person. By going after what you want rather than someone else's expectations, you live according to your own timetable. Our lives are filled with vast uncertainty, but you can be sure of one thing: The fastest way to become miserable is by trying to please everybody else.

This book is full of exercises that help you crystallize your goals and vision (for example, see Number 34). Use these to gain clarity about what's most important to you and give yourself credit for approaching your future with conscious awareness.

Explore your family roots. In this society we no longer honor our elderly, and already we're feeling the negative effects. Without a sense of continuity or history, we don't learn from what has happened before, and human life tends to lose value and meaning.

Invite your grandparents or great-grandparents to tell stories of their lives, and tape-record what they say. What important events did they live through—World War I? The Depression? What is your family's heritage—African American, European, Latino, Asian? What are the family traditions? When was the last time you all held a family reunion? **Create a family history scrapbook, in visual or oral form, and circulate it among family members.** Take pride in your roots—they're part of what make you distinctive!

40 WHY AM I SO HIGH-STRUNG?

I feel nervous, very often for no apparent reason. I'm always on edge. It's like I'm in a constant state of apprehension. I'm so tense sometimes that my whole body clenches. At times I have trouble focusing and concentrating; ordinary simple tasks can become impossible. I'm easily distracted and can become extremely irritable and impatient.

THERE'S PROBABLY a fundamental feeling that you are not in control of your environment. You believe that anything can happen at any time, anywhere. This belief can create an overwhelming sense of anxiety. It's as if you are waiting for a disaster to strike at any time, without warning. The apprehension that this creates can be almost—and sometimes is—debilitating.

You may have noticed that in a situation where you have complete control, you are generally free of anxiety. There may be anticipation and excitement, but not anxiety.

In situations where you are not in control and there is a perceived threat of danger, your anxiety level is high. It's in this state that you operate all of the time—the fight-or-flight response that normally engages during a crisis is on autopilot. Maintaining this constant and continuous anxiety state can produce health-threatening physical and psychological problems. At the very least, it produces a drain on your energy level, which leaves you feeling physically and mentally exhausted. The root of panic attacks can often be found here. Their onset is often characterized by a sense of helplessness and feeling overwhelmed.

This fundamental feeling that you are not in control of your life and circumstances comes from a lack of trust in your abilities. You doubt that you have the capabilities and capacity necessary to act in your best interest during any situation or crisis. Just as a physically weak person may fear walking alone down a dark alley, you feel equally psychologically unequipped to handle yourself.

1 **Get regular physical exercise.** Keeping your body in a constant state of fight-or-flight readiness is a quick road to burnout, fatigue, and illness. Create an outlet that siphons off your tension by finding a physical activity you enjoy enough to do regularly: brisk walking, jogging, bicycling, swimming, yoga, running, racquetball, dance, exercising at the gym. Paradoxically, one of the best ways to alleviate exhaustion at the end of a grueling workday is with a vigorous (but not overtaxing) aerobic routine or activity. Do something to get your blood pumping, and you'll move that stress right out of your system!

2 **Realize that you can't control every situation.** You can control many things, but some you can't. If you buy a present for your spouse, you can predict and hope for a favorable response, but you can't absolutely make it happen. If you have to tell your employees that a project deadline is moving up a week, you can plan ways to soften the blow, but you can't guarantee that they'll give three cheers.

Learn to roll with the punches. Do your best, then be ready to deal with whatever happens. In the words of "The Serenity Prayer" by Reinhold Niebuhr, "God, give us grace to accept with serenity the things that cannot be changed, courage to change the things which should be changed, and the wisdom to distinguish the one from the other." Commit this to memory, or write it down, and put it someplace where you will see it daily. **The next time you start to feel anxiety over something, ask yourself, "Is this something I can control?"** If it is, review your actions to see if you've done your best. If you have, relax; if you haven't, do whatever is necessary so you can rest assured. If the situation is something you can't control, however, then you must learn to embrace uncertainty. The highest level of psychological security is attained the minute you accept the unknown as part of life. Clinging to certainty and permanence is the surest route to sorrow.

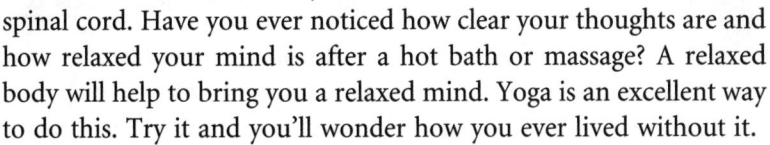 **To relax your mind you must relax your body.** We carry tension and stress in our muscles, joints, and spine. The central nervous system consists of both the brain and the spinal cord. Have you ever noticed how clear your thoughts are and how relaxed your mind is after a hot bath or massage? A relaxed body will help to bring you a relaxed mind. Yoga is an excellent way to do this. Try it and you'll wonder how you ever lived without it.

41 WHY DO I HAVE TROUBLE ASKING PEOPLE FOR HELP?

Whether it's directions or a flat tire, I'd rather do it myself than ask for help. If I'm in need of money or a ride somewhere, I'll figure out how to do it myself. Although it would be much easier if someone would help, I more often than not can't bring myself to ask. When I am offered help, I rarely accept it.

YOU WOULD RATHER SPEND five hours completing a task than ask for help and be done in twenty minutes. Your reluctance is born of one or a combination of the following. (1) You don't want to be thought of as helpless or dependent. You see asking for help as a sign of weakness. Because you question your own talents and abilities, you don't want to be perceived by others as lacking. (2) You don't want to be in debt to another and feel uncomfortable unless you can return the favor in the very near future. This discomfort comes from feelings of low self-worth; you feel undeserving of such help. (3) If you are refused help and turned down, the rejection may be too painful. You would rather believe that others would help you than be convinced otherwise. (4) Asking for help makes you feel as if you are in some way giving up or giving in. Completion of a task by yourself provides you with a sense of accomplishment. You need this because you are prone to starting many tasks and finishing very few. When things get rough you are inclined to bail out before you will seek help. You'd rather fail on your own than gain a victory that is not 100 percent yours. You need a sense of completion and independence and find it in small simple tasks. Asking others for help only reinforces your dependency with the irrational rationale, "If I can't even do this simple thing by myself, how am I ever supposed to do anything greater?"

 **Reward yourself for completing bigger and bigger tasks.** You need to move outside your comfort zone of taking on only small tasks that are easily completed by one person. Where's the challenge in always doing the familiar? Abilities need to be exercised. Unless you extend yourself, your level of competency will actually *diminish*.

Demand something better of yourself by taking on progressively bigger tasks. Do whatever is necessary to prepare for them, then carry them through to completion. If the extent of your home improvement skills has been to straighten pictures on the wall or put a new roll of toilet paper on the dispenser, do something more ambitious, such as painting the kitchen. Later you can move up to painting the whole house or remodeling the den.

Avoid the temptation to fritter away your time on a series of "little jobs." These distractions only reinforce bad habits. Instead, structure your days tightly so that a majority of your free time is devoted to the particular task you are working on. Stick to this discipline until the job is completed, then reward yourself—you've earned it!

Understand that it takes strength to ask for help. Asking people for help requires that you be willing to take a risk. It takes a strong, confident person to ask for help. There's no guarantee that the request will be granted, but if you never ask, how will you ever know? Even if you get a no answer, at least you know where the person stands, and you can move on to someone else who might be willing to answer yes.

The very act of asking makes you stronger. Several times

throughout this book (for example, Numbers 2 and 36) I urge you to ask people for help. If you haven't done these exercises, do them now. You may be amazed to find out that people have been wanting to help you all along and were waiting for you to ask. Remember, successful people don't exist in a vacuum; others helped them along the way. Those who are secure in themselves readily acknowledge the inspiration, help, and encouragement they received from those around them.

42

WHY DO I ACT CRUELLY TO PEOPLE I CARE ABOUT?

Sometimes I'm aware of it, but most times I don't realize what I'm doing. I tell a friend I'll do something that I really have no intention of doing. I put off meetings, appointments, or tasks if they're not 100 percent convenient for me. I'm capable of saying very hurtful things to people I really care about. When something goes wrong that I'm responsible for, I'm quick to blame someone or something other than myself.

Y OU'RE NOT ABLE TO ASSERT YOURSELF or express your ideas and thoughts because you either want to avoid confrontation or you do not feel that your self-interest is worthy of such a stance. Therefore, you seek to *even the score* by being hostile or cruel. Since your own desires are kept submerged, you feel, albeit unconsciously, that others' wants should not be fulfilled, either.

This may generate anger toward yourself because your own needs and wants are not being met due to your own passivity. Now the blame is directed inward, and this anger manifests in self-destructive behaviors. You now do to yourself what you have been doing to other people. You set goals you'll never reach and continually set yourself up for failure and disappointment. You procrastinate on things you want and engage in other self-destructive behaviors. Your behavior is never consciously examined because the blame for your not succeeding is sure to be placed outside yourself. Above everything else, protection of your facade is primary, and taking responsibility for your failures is not a burden you are willing to bear.

You may have noticed that when things are going well for you, you have more patience with yourself and others. When things are not going particularly well, or if you're in a bad mood, you tend to be more hostile and abrupt. The underlying current here is resentment. When your own needs are met you're willing and happy to oblige others.

1 **Express your anger in ways that don't hurt you or anyone else.** Sometimes you have a specific focus for your anger, other times not. Don't just let it build up inside; get rid of it as soon as you get a chance. Yell and scream inside your car or in the shower or while jogging. Fill a duffel bag full of old clothes or socks and punch or kick it. Go out and weed the garden, dig holes, or shovel snow. Yell at the top of your lungs while you're mowing the lawn or using a leaf blower or a snow plow, when no one can hear you anyway. Swim laps until you're good and tired. Do anything that requires heavy physical labor. If necessary, write a scathing letter to the object of your scorn, then rip it up and throw it in the trash before anybody sees it.

By venting these destructive urges, you remove the need to indulge in hostile or self-destructive behavior. Releasing your anger is an important investment in your physical, mental, and emotional health.

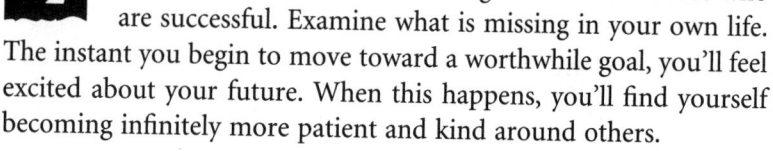

2 **Get rid of resentment by focusing on your own needs.** Happy people do not need to "get even" with those who are successful. Examine what is missing in your own life. The instant you begin to move toward a worthwhile goal, you'll feel excited about your future. When this happens, you'll find yourself becoming infinitely more patient and kind around others.

Perhaps you're resentful because you've been sacrificing your own needs for those of others. Remember that you can't take care of anyone effectively if you aren't taking care of yourself, so make sure your needs are met. Do you have time to do the things that are important to you? Are you getting enough rest and time for relaxation? Do you have opportunities to play? Do you ask people for the help you need? *Be good to yourself.*

3 **Build spiritual faith.** One way to gain meaning and purpose in life is to have an active, daily relationship with God (or divine being). Participate in your faith community and connect regularly with like-minded people, sharing joy, solace, and companionship. When you view your life within a larger context, you gain a deeper respect and appreciation for your fellow human beings as well as for life itself.

43 WHY DO I ATTRACT THE WRONG TYPE OF PERSON AND STAY IN UNHEALTHY RELATIONSHIPS?

I finally meet someone who I think is different from all the others. I'm enthusiastic about the prospect of a long-term relationship. Then little by little, I begin to find out things that I'm not quite thrilled about. In the end it turns out that this person is exactly like all of the others.

When I'm in a relationship that no longer makes me happy, I do nothing about it. I tell myself that maybe I won't find anyone better or that maybe things will change. Time passes, and nothing changes. I know that I want out, but something keeps me from leaving the relationship.

I N ALL AREAS OF LIFE, you attract not what you want but what you feel you deserve—from the job you have to where you spend your vacation to the clothes you wear. These decisions are determined by what you feel comfortable with. On a conscious level, you may feel worthy of a beautiful and fulfilling relationship; on an unconscious level, you're telling yourself a different story. When you get what you feel you deserve, you feel comfortable; when you get more than what you feel worthy of, you feel uneasy and anxious.

If you continually find yourself in unhealthy relationships, you need to review what you *want*, not what you're *used to*. It's like the man who says he would marry only an ugly woman. This way she would never cheat on him, and even if she did, he wouldn't care. Because you feel undeserving, you continue to go after and stay in relationships merely because that's what you're comfortable with. A relationship with someone you deem "perfect" causes you to be anxious.

If you to stay in a relationship that you are unhappy with, it's because you don't want to face another failure in your life. After all the effort and time put into the relationship, you don't want to admit it was a mistake. You continue to "try to make it work," and so the cycle continues. The more effort you put into making the relationship work, the harder it is to abandon your efforts. You see everything invested in the relationship as a waste.

As this cycle continues, you grow more dependent, to the point that your very identity is intertwined with this person. The end of the relationship is seen as the loss of part of yourself. This is exactly why people stay in abusive relationships. The formula is as follows: Low-self esteem clouds your judgment in choosing a partner, and then refusal to admit a mistake causes you to stay in the relationship. You're then forced to rationalize why you stay, and the only explanation you can find is that this is all you are worthy of. Your self-concept continues to diminish until you feel the only thing you do have is your lousy relationship, and you'll be damned if you lose that, too.

In the end, you attract not the person you want but the person who reinforces who you think you are. If you're unhappy with yourself, then you attract someone who makes you more unhappy. What you send out is what you get back. If you are filled with jealousy and anger, you tend to attract people with these very qualities.

Have you ever wondered why someone takes a job as a waiter in a diner when he or she could work at an expensive restaurant and earn five or six times the money? Sure, people need experience, but why wait tables for years in the same low-priced restaurant? Why not go to fancier places and earn more? Because they don't see themselves as deserving something like that. They're comfortable in their surroundings and feel they deserve to be where they are. Every day people make decisions based not on where they want to be, but where they are comfortable.

1 **Ask yourself, "What would I do if I could truly have things the way I want?"** Whom would you date? Where would you live? Where would you work? What kind of person would you be? The more difficult it is for you to come up with answers, the more desperately you need this exercise. For example, if you're stumped answering the question about whom you'd date, you've probably settled your whole life for dating anyone who shows an interest in you, rather than having the confidence to approach people you actually like.

Create a poster, chart, or other visual representation of your desires and put it where you can see it every day. Find pictures in magazines or catalogs of people you find physically attractive and cut them out for your poster. Add words to represent qualities that are important in a romantic mate, such as "loving," "honest," "affectionate," and "sexy." Add pictures of activities you would enjoy doing with this person.

Don't confine this exercise to romantic relationships. Do it for wealth, health, creativity, and other important areas of your life. *Gain confidence in stating and visualizing your desires and get ready for them to become a reality.*

2 **Like yourself more, and others will respond in kind.** The better you feel about yourself, the more people will be attracted to you. When folks meet you for the first time, they have no idea what you're like. If you send them the message that you're worthless—by mumbling, standing with a slumped posture, not looking them in the eyes, saying negative things about yourself—they assume you know whereof you speak and tend to avoid you.

The best way to attract friendly, outgoing, likable people is to be one yourself. Try standing up straighter, looking people directly in the eyes, and smiling. Move outside your comfort zone; go to a party or gathering where you don't know anyone and spend at least a half hour mixing. It *is* a party, right? So you've got to assume that other people are there to be sociable. Distinguish yourself by demonstrating the most important conversational skill of all: being a good listener.

44

WHY DO I ENJOY GOSSIPING SO MUCH?

There's nothing I enjoy more than spreading a little news around the water cooler. I get right on the phone to tell someone the "latest," and I'm excited when I have an opportunity to share some "dirt" and do so every chance I get. I read the gossip columns with enthusiasm and share news about people I don't even know. I also have trouble keeping a secret.

WHILE WE CAN ALL BE GUILTY of this pastime every once in a while, there are those who thrive on gossip. If you live to tell people *the latest*, you do so for one or more of the following reasons. (1) The misdeeds of others offer you an opportunity to feel better about your own behavior, which you may not be proud of. (2) By discussing the lives of other people you don't have to face the perils in your own life. Shifting the spotlight away from yourself is preferable to facing your own situation. (3) Gossiping gives you a sense of power. You know something that somebody else doesn't. You feel in a position of authority by being the one who provides this new information. Others will come to you for information, giving you a feeling of prestige and importance. You are undoubtedly the person who has to give "hints" about birthday presents and surprise parties. You beam with pride as a captivated audience hangs on your every word, eager to hear your newly acquired knowledge. This is just like children who can often be heard saying, "I know something you don't know." (4) Sometimes you need an outlet for negative feelings you have toward yourself. You're unable to deal with them consciously, so they manifest into unkind stories about others.

 **Forgive yourself for past mistakes and rededicate yourself to your goals.** We've all behaved in ways we're not proud of, so stop letting your shame and regret drive your current behavior. There's no need to build yourself up by tearing others down. Simply shift your focus from the negative to the positive.

Review any incidents in your past that you're particularly ashamed of and remind yourself that you were doing the best you could with the resources you had at the time. Put these incidents to rest in whatever way will really impress it on your unconscious. For example, you could write them down on paper, then burn it.

Lift your focus from the mundane to the sublime. Avoid TV shows, tabloids, and magazines that sensationalize the baser aspects of human behavior. Instead, read stories about people who rose above ordinary circumstances to accomplish great things. More and more success books are being published, and you can read about great figures of the past in your local library. Patronize movies, plays, and other cultural events that elevate the human spirit.

Practice self-restraint. Great minds talk about ideas, average minds talk about things, and small minds talk about people. The next time you feel the urge to dish out the latest dirt, ask yourself, "Who will benefit from this?" If it's not the person you're talking to or the person you're speaking about, don't do it.

If this proves too difficult, sterner measures are called for. Write twenty-five times, "I gossiped about [the person's name]," and post it where people can see it, then apologize personally to the person.

Feed $1 into a penalty jar, and when there's enough money, buy something for the people you've gossiped about, explaining to them how so much money accumulated. Put off by a day or a week your next vacation.

All of these are strong medicine, but if you do any of them even once, that's usually enough to break you permanently of the habit.

45

WHY DO I ENJOY HEARING THE SECRETS AND CONFESSIONS OF OTHERS?

Walking by a room, I stop for a moment to listen to a heated conversation going on inside. Even thoroughly uninteresting information can command my attention, as I listen intently to the woman explain to the assistant manager of the supermarket why she needs to return a can of tomato soup.

W E ALL HAVE A LITTLE VOYEURISM in us, whether it's listening in on conversations or watching others. But if your preoccupation extends beyond occasional interest in the trivialities of other people's lives, then the following is an explanation of this response.

Seeing slices of other people's lives provides the comfort of knowing that you're not alone with your quirks and neuroticisms, you're not the only one who has regrets, insecurities, and problems. Knowing that you are not the only one with a *dark side* makes you feel better about your own impulses and beliefs.

Hearing the confessions and secrets of others is like a verbal car accident. It's intriguing to see what it's like when things don't go well for other people. You're comforted to know that as bad as things get, at least it's not *you* in that situation.

If your "curiosity" is anxiety driven, then your thirst for information is motivated by the unconscious desire to collect information that you feel you may need. Underlying your curiosity is the desire to collect knowledge that you can apply and use in other aspects of your life. You don't know what may happen next, so you want to be armed with as much information as you can gather.

Get busier with your own pursuits. When you're occupied with something going on in your own life, you are much less apt to become intrigued with the lives of other people. Chances are either that you are not filling your spare time productively enough or that you're working too hard and not giving yourself any recreation time at all, causing you to seek instant relief by listening to the conversations of others. The solution to both these tendencies is to take up a hobby, since hobbies focus our energies while allowing us to relax and work at our own pace.

Without at least some recreation, we become too fixed in our routine—and rigidity tends to dull mental acuity. Do something that offers a lot of contrast to what you do during a typical workday. If you are an accountant, take up a physical sport such as street hockey or one-on-one basketball. If you work on car transmissions all day, take an adult education course at night. Or introduce yourself to a discipline that has mental *and* physical benefits, such as a martial art (kung fu, karate, aikido), archery, target shooting, or fencing.

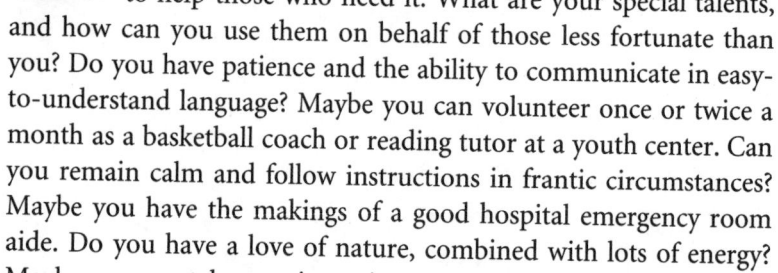

Develop compassion for others. Channel an unhealthy fascination for other people's "dirty laundry" into efforts to help those who need it. What are your special talents, and how can you use them on behalf of those less fortunate than you? Do you have patience and the ability to communicate in easy-to-understand language? Maybe you can volunteer once or twice a month as a basketball coach or reading tutor at a youth center. Can you remain calm and follow instructions in frantic circumstances? Maybe you have the makings of a good hospital emergency room aide. Do you have a love of nature, combined with lots of energy? Maybe you can take part in environmental cleanup efforts, or train to become a park ranger's assistant in a national wildlife preserve.

By giving to others, you give to yourself. No longer do you listen to other people's secrets and feel guilty about it. Instead, you feel the deep satisfaction and joy of making a positive difference in the life of another human being.

46 WHY AM I PLAGUED BY SELF-DOUBT?

I constantly question my ability and talent. While I feel deep down inside that I am an intelligent and capable person, when I'm in the middle of something—a tennis match or a meeting—I suddenly get the thought, Maybe I can't. *I keep from thinking of things I would like to do because I know it's just so far out of my reach. I think I'm confident and secure overall, but at some level I feel I'll mess up whatever I do.*

E VERYTHING WE DO IS CONSISTENT with our self-image. What we think of ourself dictates our behavior, thoughts, beliefs, and feelings. The governing distinction between those with a positive self-image and those with a negative self-image is that the former do not associate poor performance with being a bad person. Those with a poor self-image internalize all outcomes, even those over which they have very little or no control. For this reason you rarely go outside your field of competence and see little point in challenging yourself with new opportunities.

You're in the habit of remembering only your failures and focusing on what you did wrong, not what you did right. When victorious in competition, you become convinced that your opponent let you win or was having an off day; you rarely ascribe success to your own skill or talent. Any success you do have is attributed to good luck or circumstance. You do not take credit for your achievements but readily accept blame for your failures.

While on a conscious level you recognize that you can't be good at everything, you expand a specific deficiency to envelop your entire self-image. In other words, a poor self-image in one area of your life manifests into a general sense of low self-esteem. At some point in your development, you lacked a positive source from which to draw. A low level of confidence in one area was allowed to spread and become a general self-image that you formed. Those who excel in at least one area of their life can often accept less than great attributes as isolated characteristics. You see negative traits and use them as the basis for personal identity.

If you do have a source of pride, it's likely to have been placed on a single trait, usually something superficial, such as appearance. When you have cause to question your perception of this trait, it brings into question your entire self-worth. In other words, you put all your psychological eggs into a very transitory and fragile basket.

Overall demeanor differs based on individuality type. The introvert becomes even more withdrawn and craves anonymity. The extrovert tends to crave attention to compensate for a lack of perceived presence. This is the person who has the volume turned up all the way on the car radio.

At one time or another we all doubt ourselves, our abilities, our intentions, our goals—anything that can be doubted often is. The main question is whether we let these passing doubts continue on their way or whether we grab hold of them and let them take root. Everybody has strengths and everyone has weaknesses. This is an undeniable truth.

Tomorrow, write down *everything* you do well. Instead of pouncing on yourself for every perceived mistake, make special note of anything that you do successfully. When you give your children a hug before sending them off to school, congratulate yourself on being a loving, demonstrative parent. When you arrive at work on time, acknowledge your reliability and punctuality. When you make someone else smile or laugh, silently applaud your sense of humor. When you conduct a great meeting, write a persuasive report, solve a problem, or simply enjoy your work, write it down. For every accomplishment during the day, no matter how small or seemingly insignificant, make a mental and written note to yourself.

Once a week for the next month, make a new list. At the end of the month, when you review your four lists, you'll notice some recurring areas where you have obvious talents and skills. Now that you know what they are, you can focus on enhancing them, making conscious choices to act on your innate abilities whenever you have the chance.

2 **Whenever you begin to doubt yourself, acknowledge and accept your weaknesses.** When those moments of self-doubt arrive (and they do for everyone), just say to yourself, "My backhand could be improved," or "I could use more confidence when I'm talking with people," or whatever is a simple statement of the difficulty you're having. Don't dwell on the feelings, and don't generalize; statements like "I'm completely inadequate" or "I always screw up" are too general (and inaccurate).

By simply *accepting* your weaknesses you allow yourself to be consciously aware of them without beating yourself up. If you allow yourself to be mired in the emotions that attend your so-called inadequacies, you will not be motivated to change them; the feelings are too debilitating. But if you can become matter-of-fact and accepting about areas that could use some improvement, then you'll find yourself coming up with practical and doable solutions—solutions you'll be motivated to follow through on.

3 **Try something new.** Allow yourself to be a beginner in something. Learn a language, start playing a new sport, study geography, take up gourmet cooking. Enjoy your inexperience! Think how much you will have gained in just a few weeks or months and learn to appreciate it whenever you discover something new that can be improved on.

47 WHY DO I NEED TO BE REASSURED THAT I'M LOVED AND CARED ABOUT?

I keep saying "I love you" almost to the point of nausea, and I get upset if I don't hear it back every time. I'm constantly asking others, "What's wrong?" or "Are you mad at me?" At times I feel abandoned by the whole world and rejected by all the people I love and care for.

Y OUR NEED FOR CONSTANT REASSURANCE over the status of your relationship is at the very least a matter of insecurity. Specifically, this feeling is generated because you feel undeserving of your partner. This perceived imbalance causes you constantly to assess your status in the relationship for signs that the other person has *caught on.*

You need constant reassurance that everything is okay, because you feel that the other person is getting the proverbial short end of the stick. You question and analyze every conversation for a hidden meaning. This lack of perspective does not allow you to place small disagreements in their proper place, within the scope and context of the entire relationship. You blow things out of proportion because you judge the soundness of your relationship on what is happening from minute to minute. All the love that you've received to that point is not factored into the equation. All you see is someone who said something hurtful, which translates into the fact that this person no longer cares about you. You're prone to overreacting to everything said because you place so much emphasis on what is happening *now*. If a small argument follows, then you reevaluate the entire relationship and conclude, at least temporarily, that it is irrevocably damaged.

You'll say "I love you" five times in a conversation and get upset if you hear it back only four times. Because you are always questioning the status of your relationship, you need to be constantly reassured. You may even resort to testing your partner with little requests and favors just to "make sure."

1 **Instead of constantly verbalizing your love, be content just to feel it.** Whenever you feel the urge to tell someone "I love you," take a deep breath and just feel your love for that person—don't say a word. Take a reading on your intentions: Ask yourself, "Was I feeling incredibly *loving* just now, or *needy*?" Being able to identify the difference is half the battle toward being more truthful both with yourself and others in relationships.

2 **Learn to express love to *yourself*.** Do you hold yourself up to a standard that you can never satisfy? When you love yourself and accept yourself as you are, then you naturally expect others to do the same. But if you're always picking out faults and shortcomings, you feel others are as well. The important thing to remember is that in the gap between reality and your perception of reality lies a miserable place. To close the gap you need to see yourself for who you are, the good and the bad. In seeing, there is acceptance. In acceptance, there is love.

48 WHY DO COMPLIMENTS AND PRAISE MAKE ME UNCOMFORTABLE?

I feel uneasy when I'm praised for my performance or appearance.
When I am complimented, I feel that someone is just being nice.
When I do a good job, I shy away from recognition and praise.
It makes me feel good to be complimented but uneasy at the same
time.

HOW YOU HANDLE A COMPLIMENT tells a lot about you. Denying a compliment often comes from feeling unworthy of praise. When you suffer from low self-esteem, compliments are craved on one level yet dismissed on another. You want to be appreciated and told that you look nice or do good work. But when praised for your efforts, you respond with, "Anyone could have done it" or "Are you kidding?" Of course there's such a thing as humility and grace in accepting a compliment. But becoming flustered and frightened by genuine praise is due to feelings of unworth. You usually feel more comfortable being praised for what you do, than for who you are. If someone tells you that she likes your shirt, you might thank her. But if you're told that the shirt looks good on you, you're inclined to fluff off the compliment. You may become uncomfortable when people are too nice to you. The extra polite waiter makes you feel uneasy because you feel that this type of service is wasted on you.

1 **Say "thank you"—no less, no more.** Whether someone lavishes you with "exaggerated" praise or merely admires your outfit, graciously answer, "Thank you." It doesn't matter whether you think it's empty or misguided flattery; if someone offers you praise, take it! Think of it as if you were traveling in a country where it is incredibly impolite not to accept an invitation that is made to you. In the same way, it is ungrateful and selfish not to accept the compliments people offer us: They are lovely "invitations" to appreciate the gesture—and ourselves.

2 **Don't fish for compliments by belittling yourself.** Criticizing yourself just to give others an opportunity to "correct" you and offer praise and accolades is a dishonest and ultimately degrading process. Not only do people catch on pretty quickly, but they also might begin to believe your "false advertising." Tell them how lousy you are at your job, how seldom you follow through, how you can never get anything right, what a loser you are—and chances are that you will actually become known for those traits.

3 **Compliment other people.** How often do you tell other people that you admire them? Doing this is a great way to learn how other people graciously accept compliments and to beef up your own skill in letting others know that they are appreciated. Use phrases like, "I really admire the way you . . ." "I would love to learn how you . . ." "You are incredibly . . ." "I've never seen anyone who could . . ."

Use your imagination! Most people love to receive sincere compliments.

49

WHY DO I FEEL GUILTY FOR THINGS BEYOND MY CONTROL?

At some level I blame myself for earthquakes, rainstorms, and all the world's problems. I feel responsible for events that are beyond my control or for things that I have nothing to do with.

Y OU ARE SO LADEN WITH GUILT that you feel guilty for the things you do and guilty for the things you don't do. These feelings of guilt are manifestations of a conflict between the actual self and the ideal self—a conflict between what you do and what you feel you should do, what you've done and what you feel you should have done, what you would like to do and what you feel you need to do.

Guilt is the anger you feel toward yourself. If these feelings are not dealt with, the guilt can overwhelm you to the point of depression. Guilty feelings are often met with self-deprivation or self-punishment. This is how you get back at yourself. You feel you must make retribution for the wrongs you have done or for the rights you have not.

The cause for this behavior is rarely consciously examined but is consciously rationalized with statements to yourself such as, "I don't have time for myself" and "It's not really worth it." In essence, though, what you're saying is that *you* are not really worth the time.

You are apt to renounce competition, as these feelings inhibit the competitive spirit. You don't want to "beat" anybody because you feel unworthy of winning and feel badly for making your opponent lose. Competition produces a no-win situation. If you lose, you're a loser. If you win, you feel guilty.

Sometimes we do things that we feel guilty about but are unwilling consciously to examine our actions. Instead we take responsibility for the near extinction of the white leopard. Guilt can gnaw away at our inner being. It's a terribly destructive force because it offers no benefit and destroys all in its path. It's easy to say "Don't feel guilty"—but not so easy to do. However, punishing yourself does not change a thing.

1 Do something. If you can do something about the situation you feel guilty about, then by all means, do it! If you feel guilty for having missed your mother's birthday, call her and send a gift. If you feel guilty about the overpopulation of the earth, commit to zero population growth and initiate discussions about it with friends. If you feel guilty about making your little sister feel bad when you were children, apologize now. Of course, if you feel guilty about something you can't do anything about . . .

2 Let go and build your strength for changing what you can. Remember "The Serenity Prayer": "God, give us grace to accept with serenity the things that cannot be changed, courage to change the things which should be changed, and the wisdom to distinguish the one from the other." When you begin to feel guilty about something, recognize that this means you *care* but not necessarily that you are *responsible*. By releasing yourself from this heavy burden, you can use your strength to make a difference instead of carrying the dead weight of guilt.

50 WHY DO I APOLOGIZE EVEN WHEN IT'S NOT MY FAULT?

I apologize for the things I did and for what I didn't do. I'm constantly explaining my actions to others and justifying them to myself. I feel awful when I can't come through for someone, and I try as hard as I can to make up for anything I've done that may have offended anyone. I'm constantly anxious that I'll do something wrong or injurious to another.

I F YOU'RE ALWAYS APOLOGIZING, you either are doing many things you shouldn't be doing or you are feeling guilty for no real reason. You apologize for the things you do and for the things you haven't done but feel that you should have.

You have a need to avoid confrontation, so you are quick to apologize. The course of least resistance is the road you prefer to take. You're uncomfortable defending your views and opinions so you submit to the ideas of others.

You have an underlying belief that your worth is determined by what you can do for other people. Your value as a person is based on how valuable you are to others. When you are helpful and productive for others, then you feel good about yourself. The flip side is that you feel terrible if you don't come through for anyone who asks for your help.

 **Stand up for yourself.** Eleanor Roosevelt once said, "No one can make you feel inferior without your consent." Don't offer up your dignity to compensate for minor inconveniences. Sadly, in this world there are people who try to make you feel terrible about the slightest unexpected incident. Don't let them have your self-respect—it's hard to get it back. And remember, the only way they can take it is if you give it to them.

Don't overapologize. Refrain from saying things like, "I'm so sorry," "It will never happen again," and "Please forgive me," when a simple "That's not what I intended" will suffice.

Do apologize when it's appropriate. It's completely appropriate to say you're sorry when you've seriously hurt someone. But there's a clear distinction between blaming yourself for other people's misunderstandings and attempting to comfort someone who is upset. Just ask yourself, "Did I *cause* this to happen, or was I simply nearby?"

51 WHY AM I SO SUPERSTITIOUS?

When I walk down the street, I'm careful to avoid the cracks in the sidewalk, while making sure my left foot lands entirely inside the cement square. I have to say "take care" at the end of every conversation and knock on wood when discussing my health or good fortune. If I'm gambling or playing sports I do the same set of rituals every time.

MANY PEOPLE ARE a little superstitious, but your life is ruled by rituals or beliefs that have no basis in fact. While this behavior is anxiety driven, the cause of the actual anxiety is your fundamental feeling of not being in control or in charge of your life. It's likely that you have, to some degree, lost the capacity to distinguish between what you can control and what you cannot. If you were in control of your life, you would see, every day, examples of your actions producing specific results. Without this control, you begin to lose the understanding of this connection. The correlation between cause and effect is blurred. You've lost the ability to distinguish between those things that happen to you and those that you make happen. This can make you a virtual slave to rituals and compulsive behaviors. You need to have some sense of control, so you draw your own correlation between an event and a behavior. This makes you feel as if you're more in control. If you knock three times on your head, your spouse will get home from work safely. Your actions give you the illusion of control.

Many things happen in your life that you have no explanation for, but you need to attribute them to something. So you continue with your rituals. You're afraid something bad will happen or you won't get the same results if you don't continue with the behavior. So you keep at it, even though you know it is ridiculous.

1 **If you feel like you've lost control of your life, reestablish the relationship between cause and effect.** There's nothing like setting and achieving a goal for giving you a sense of power and control in your life. If you've ever lost weight, finished college, climbed a mountain, learned to dance, or done any goal-oriented activity, you know what a huge boon this is. It proves that when you set your mind on something, there's no stopping you: You *do* have control over the most important thing in your life—*you*.

For ten minutes, brainstorm what you'd love to learn, have, give, and do in your life. No limits! Don't worry about whether you could actually achieve any of these things. Just let yourself imagine. Whom would you meet? Where would you go? What would you buy? How could you contribute to someone else's life? Write as quickly as you can, and dream big!

When your ten minutes are up, take a look at your list. Which goal could you achieve this year if you absolutely set your heart on it? **Write this goal at the top of a clean sheet of paper.** Underneath it, write three things you could do this month toward its attainment. Now write three things you could do *today* toward its attainment. Pick one of these three things and do it! Next week, do one more. In the third week, do one more. And in the fourth week, pick one of your ideas to do for the month.

At this point, you have a choice. Do you want to really go for it? By now you will have seen that you are making real progress, that your actions produce results in your life. Continue to follow your plan and you will achieve your goal in one year! Earl Nightingale in his classic *The Strangest Secret*, put it best when he said, "You become what you think about." Your thoughts are responsible for where you are today. If you want to be in a different place tomorrow, simply change your thinking.

Realize that there are some things in life that, no matter how hard we try, we can't control. We can't control the weather, the way other people behave, or the stock market. This should not stop you from making decisions and taking action on things that you can control. The only certainty in life is that nothing is certain. But this doesn't mean you should throw up your hands and let lady luck deal out your destiny.

52

WHY AM I SO CONCERNED ABOUT THE OPINIONS OF OTHER PEOPLE?

A passing glance from someone I don't even know occupies my thoughts for the entire day. I'm told that my face looks a little full, and my whole week is ruined. I'm always asking others what they think of my ideas, my performance, and my appearance. Even opinions from people whom I don't like or respect weigh heavily on my mind.

T HE TRUTH IS THAT almost everyone cares what other people think. This is what helps to make public speaking the number-one fear. But if *your* opinion of yourself changes based upon other people's comments, then you are relinquishing your greatest power.

The one thing we all have complete and total control over is our thoughts. And it is our thoughts that determine everything else in our life. If you give away that power, you give away the control of your very life. Your happiness and self-worth are then placed in the hands of other people. Your mood becomes a swinging pendulum. Somebody says something nice, and you're in a good mood. Somebody says something negative, and you're in a bad mood.

The more you care what you think of yourself, the less you care what other people think of you. Consequently, the less confident you are in your own opinion, the more heavily you weigh the opinions of others. Because of this, you do things you don't want to do and don't do things that you want to do, to avoid any criticism.

A major distinction lies between *wanting* people to like you and *needing* people to like you. Consequently, you are easily manipulated by others. You do things you don't want to do because of a need for approval and recognition. Your actions become defined by the type of praise you receive from others, not the pride you get from yourself. This is not living; this is not life. In the end, others control more than just your mood, they control your very life; your destiny is put into the hands of strangers.

Your mood and emotions are subject to the whims and words of others. Your state of mind, whether happy or sad, is dependent on what others say or don't say. Your true self is very different from the image you create for others so they will love you. In the exchange, you lose yourself, molding to the image created and demanded by others.

Being hypersensitive to public perception extends to a myriad of behaviors and beliefs. You are easily embarrassed in social settings; you would never dream of parking illegally in a tow-away zone; you would never hold up a line at the supermarket over a price discrepancy. You are far more likely to remember negative things said about you than positive. Since positive statements are inconsistent with your own feelings about yourself, they are filtered out, and only negative images, which are consistent with your own self-image, come through. You often review past conversations over and over in your head to see how you might have been perceived and how well you came across. You are highly reluctant to eat out by yourself, especially dinner, because you don't want others to think that you do not have any friends.

Obsessive concern with the opinions of others can lead to the "island syndrome." This happens when your life is dictated greatly by external influences and opinions. You fantasize about being stranded on a desert island or about being the last person left on Earth. In these scenarios you're released from the confinement of public perception.

You subject your mind to every unpredictable influence—mentally digesting the comments and behaviors of the rest of the world.

1 **Just say no.** The next time you don't really want to do something that someone else has asked you to do, decline politely. Then go out and treat yourself! In other words, learn to express your honest feelings by telling other people the truth when they ask, "Would you like to . . . ?" Every time you do this, give yourself a reward, whether that means buying yourself a little present or indulging yourself in some other way. (You might even consider making the exercise below your reward.) This will help you to feel good about telling the truth and not doing "favors" for people when you really don't want to. Most people would rather you never did them this type of favor, anyway.

2 **Go out to dinner by yourself and take a good book or a magazine that you enjoy.** Pick a restaurant you love. And when the host asks you, "How many?" be sure to smile broadly as you respond, "One, please. I'm treating myself tonight." Order your favorite foods and eat s-l-o-w-l-y, savoring every bite, reading whenever you feel like it. Turn your evening into a "date" with yourself; the only one you have to impress is *you*.

3 **Give yourself a reality check.** The next time you are faced with a decision, ask yourself, "If I lived in a foreign country, without my family or friends, would I still make the same decision?" This question helps to filter out any influence that others may have on your decision. It helps you to become aware of just how much of your life is dictated by the opinions of others.

53

WHY DON'T I ASSERT MYSELF WHEN I REALLY NEED TO?

It's been fifteen minutes, and the server hasn't come over to my table. Although I'm starving, I don't want to be a bother. I'm in line and five people cut right in front of me, but I decide not to make a scene. My newspaper is always late and wet; the neighbor next door has her camper parked half on my lawn, and the cashier rang up the wrong price. But I figure "it's not worth it" and "I'll let it go," because it "really doesn't bother me."

Y OUR LACK OF ASSERTIVENESS is driven by a fundamental fear of being chastised or punished for expressing yourself. You're not one to rock the boat or to make a scene, because you are afraid that other people will think poorly of you.

If you are in a restaurant and do not see your server for fifteen minutes, you may not complain. However, if you had not eaten in two days, you would certainly object to the slow service. You would no longer care what others thought of you or your actions. While you may not feel worthy of proper service, you do feel worthy of not starving to death. Clearly, assertiveness is not a matter of not *having it in you*. It's merely a matter of bringing it out. The degree to which you assert yourself is in direct relation to the value you place on yourself. The more valuable a person you believe yourself to be, then the more justified you feel in representing your best interests.

Sometimes those with low self-esteem can be seen as very assertive. While similar results may occur, this behavior can be more appropriately defined as *aggression*. Assertiveness comes out of self-love and an interest in fostering your own well-being. Aggression comes from anger or fear. Have you ever noticed that when you are in a really bad mood and feeling angry with the world, you take on a more assertive posture? You are focused on this feeling and your situation, so the opinions of other people take a back seat to your anger.

Ask for the works. Go to a full-service gas station, get one dollar's worth of gas, and ask the attendant to clean your windshield. If your initial thought is, *Oh, I could never do that*, then you really need to do this! What's the very worst that could happen? As you pull away, he mutters under his breath some unflattering remark? Big deal. Just this simple activity can renew and awaken a great sense of personal empowerment.

Take it back. Purposely buy something you don't need at a store you know will take returns. Wait one week, then return the item—tags still on, unused—to the store. Tell the clerk that you simply don't want it. No other reason. No exchange. After you leave the store, use the cash to buy something you'd really like somewhere else!

Take an objective look. When you find yourself unwilling to claim your best interests, ask yourself the following questions. (1) What am I worth? (2) Will I be glad that I took action when I think about this later? (3) What's the very worst that could happen? (4) Will this make me stronger or weaker?

54 WHY DO I FEEL AS IF NOTHING WILL EVER MAKE ME HAPPY?

I have a feeling of hopelessness that just won't go away. I try different things, but I remain unfulfilled and uninspired. At times I'm so bored I think I'm going to go out of my mind. I can't find enjoyment or a sense of purpose in life. I'm not able to enjoy things that should be enjoyable. And I'm finding that fewer and fewer things actually give me pleasure.

I F YOU SUDDENLY acquired the power of invisibility you would probably be elated. However, let's say that you find out that every other person on the planet not only can make themselves invisible, but they can also fly. Now you're not so happy; in fact, you feel shortchanged. You can't even enjoy your new gift because you're mad.

This example reflects your thinking with most aspects of your life. Your mind dwells on what you don't have, not on what you do. Your thoughts are not on where you are but on where you are not. Because you're unable to enjoy what you have, you're mind is filled with petty concerns and distractions.

You're not able to enjoy life because you're not able to enjoy *the things* in life. It's really that simple. Stemming from an inability to give your attention to a given situation, your mind is constantly wandering from the past to the future but gliding over the present. You've lost the ability to experience anything fully, without distraction. Your mind takes you away from what you should be enjoying. When eating a meal, instead of enjoying each bite and savoring the flavor, you're thinking about the meeting you had earlier.

Finding it increasingly difficult to derive pleasure from things, you exaggerate the discomfort in experiences, so that the contrast to pleasure is greater. For example, you might not take your shoes off, even if they hurt, because the longer the duration of the discomfort, the greater the pleasure will seem.

Happiness is not something that can be gained or acquired. It can't be searched for or *discovered*. Happiness can only be *uncovered*. That elusive destination is not "out there" but inside, ready to be released. You certainly can't create happiness by repeating to yourself, "I am happy."

This is a difficult cycle from which to break free. When you're feeling down, your very attempt to feel better usually makes you feel worse. While you try to do fun things, you derive little enjoyment because the events are isolated. You aren't able to enjoy yourself because you know you will be let down when it's over, and you don't want to have too much fun. You also place too much emphasis on the event because it's one of the few opportunities you have for enjoyment. This creates pressure and anxiety when it should be relaxing and enjoyable. The very reason you are sad in the first place is because you have met with disappointment. You don't want to set yourself up for additional disappointment, so you don't seek out new opportunities for growth and enjoyment.

As long as there's a gap between where you are and where you feel you should be, you will be unhappy. On a weekend you are probably in a better mood than during the week, even if your activity is the same. The difference is that on the weekend, *you're not supposed to be doing something else*, so you are free to enjoy your activity without guilt. During the week, you feel you should be working toward something else.

Just for now, give up all of your goals and plans for yourself and your life. Don't try to be anything more than what you are. And know that it's okay just to be, without doing. We are, after all, human beings, not human doings. Releasing yourself from this burden of "I must . . ." allows you to focus on where you are now. Once you are content with where you are today, you can start to make plans for tomorrow.

Help a stranger. The quickest and best way to quit feeling sorry for yourself is to focus on someone else's needs. Direct your energies toward coming up with solutions for another person's problems or concerns. Go as far outside your normal realm as possible. If you rarely venture into the inner city, do it now. Offer your services at a youth center, helping the staff or interacting with the teenagers who use the facility. If your workday is typically fast paced, spend time at a nursing home and visit with the elderly citizens who live there. One of the greatest gifts you can offer is simply to *listen to them*, letting them know that you're another human being who cares whether they live or die.

Every day, for just a few minutes, embrace the notion that you're done struggling and done trying to be someone else. This puts balance into your life and allows you to enjoy where you are and pursue only what you really want to. When you cease to struggle with where you should be, then you can enjoy where you are.

55 WHY IS THERE SO MUCH DISAPPOINTMENT IN MY LIFE?

Even if something goes better than I could have hoped for, I'm left feeling disappointed when it's over. When the fun ends, depression sets in. Sometimes I feel as if nothing ever goes my way, and I can't get a decent break in life. I have trouble enjoying things because I know that when they're over, I'll be saddened.

ANYONE WHO TRIES to hold on to pleasure is bound to wind up disappointed in the end. The cause of most disappointment is trying to give permanence to the temporary. Since all things in life are transitory, you are continually disappointed.

You have a need to believe that there is such a thing as permanence. In craving stability and security, you do not accept and recognize the transitory nature of your world. So you create things that you can cling to—beliefs, ideals, and judgments—and you hold fast to them. But this is not living; it is only a response to fear.

When you do have a pleasurable experience, your mind craves the opportunity to recapture the sensation. Waiting for a chance to repeat the experience, your life becomes rigid and habitual because you deprive yourself of the ability to pursue other outlets for your pleasure. You go with what you know and what you like, greatly decreasing the possibility for disappointment but consequently greatly limiting your freedom and happiness.

You may be the type of person who never wants things to be "just right." The pain that comes from losing whatever it is would be too great. When moving into a new apartment, you leave some things undone to make sure that it's not perfect. This is your way of lessening the blow and the letdown when the time comes to move out. Because of this you have trouble fully enjoying yourself. You're never really happy. Anything you have in your life that brings happiness only becomes a source of tomorrow's pain and suffering. But the reality of life is that what makes us happy now may not be here tomorrow. And for you, the pain of losing what you enjoy is far greater than any pleasure you could derive from it. This is because your *fear* of losing that which you enjoy prevents you from fully experiencing the joy.

Another source of your disappointment can be found in setting unrealistic expectations and goals that can never be reached. Having unreachable plans means that you're continually setting yourself up for failure and disappointment. Your imagination stretches beyond the grasp of your reality, where your ideals can never be met.

 **Start living in the moment.** Instead of constantly looking back on what has happened in the past—both good and bad—or looking into the future for what may happen, focus on where you are *right now*.

Try this experiment over the next week for two hours a day. First, set a timer for two hours. Until the timer goes off, any time you start to think about anything other than the present, put a check mark on a piece of paper, then redirect your thoughts to whatever you are doing *in that moment*. If you catch yourself thinking about when the timer will go off, put a check mark. If you start thinking about things you ought to do when the experiment is over for the day, put a check mark. If you begin reliving what you had for lunch, put a check mark. *Stay in the present.* Each day, try to reduce the number of check marks on the page. At the end of the week, you should see a huge improvement.

2   **Accept that everything in life is transitory.** In some cases, this is a blessing; in others it can be painful. Yet it is an undeniable fact of life that nothing lasts forever, so your best tactic is to respond to events *as they are happening*, not in advance and not long after the fact. This is not to say that you shouldn't plan for what you know will happen, simply that you shouldn't torture yourself with what *might* happen. Make reasonable plans, but enjoy the moment!

56 WHY AM I SO QUICK TO JUDGE OTHER PEOPLE?

I'm quick to judge people for anything and everything. I don't even realize the number of times during the day that I pass judgment on people and things I know very little about. I make blanket statements, often without examining the specific instance. I often judge others by their actions but myself by my intentions.

E ACH DAY YOU MAKE literally hundreds if not thousands of decisions, everything from what to wear to what to say. Some of these decisions take barely a fraction of a second to make, while others can be deliberated over for minutes, hours, days, weeks, months, years, and even a lifetime. If you didn't have a way of grouping information, prioritizing, and cataloging your world, you would spend all of your time deliberating over every little decision. So grouping information is essential to exist in the world. But this process too often extends to instances where independent inspection of the facts is necessary. And you become so used to making assumptions without adequate information that you cannot see what *is*.

This behavior is nurtured by insecurity. You need to insulate yourself with ideas and concepts you feel comfortable with. You barricade yourself in with your beliefs and defend against those on the outside who threaten you and your position. These attitudes and beliefs are a manifestation of your ego. The sole purpose of the ego is to perpetuate itself. It craves continuity. It's unsettling to a fragile self to believe that what it holds to be true may be in question. There's no need to spoil your mood by taking the time and pain to weigh the evidence. Instead you can rely on a convenient stereotype and not bother to examine the facts.

You have a tendency to see people, situations, and ideas in black and white. For you, there is no gray area in which opposing ideas can coexist. There is a winner and there is a loser. There is a right and there is a wrong. Since you need to be right, you must make all opposing sides wrong. As the saying goes, "When the other is wrong, I feel strong." You have a fundamental insecurity about who you are and where you stand. You seek to carve out an identity for yourself by placing labels on others.

You often have a need to label your emotions. Like the world, your mind is cluttered and needs to be organized, often at the expense of individual inspection. You're quick to say, "I'm in a mild depression" or "I feel like I'm getting sick." In doing this, it takes the pressure off not knowing how you feel. You have formed a conclusion and now you do everything in your power to see that it does, in fact, become your reality. The danger in this is clear.

1 **Consider the opposite viewpoint.** The next time you make a snap judgment about a situation, take a few moments to understand an opposing viewpoint. If you've jumped to a conclusion, ask yourself, "What have I overlooked? What have I failed even to notice? What if my perceptions are completely inaccurate? What is the cost of misjudging this situation?"

2 **Put yourself in someone else's shoes.** There's no better way to break this habit of judging than to put yourself in the other person's shoes. There are always two sides to a story, so try not to form an opinion until you hear them both. You wouldn't want people to judge you without getting your side of the story. Imagine a legal system in which the defendant never got a chance to defend himself or herself. Give other people the benefit of the doubt. You will find that empathy gives you great strength. It empowers you in ways that you can't even imagine. The understanding that you gain gives you a complete sense of control, almost a godlike feeling. Try it today and see if you don't come alive.

3 **See if you can go through an entire day without forming an opinion.** Try not to judge people or situations as either good or bad. Warning: This exercise is impossible to do perfectly the first time you try it; people are decision makers by nature. But this will really wake you up to just how often you draw conclusions based on insufficient information.

57 WHY IS IT THAT THE BETTER THINGS ARE GOING THE WORSE I FEEL?

I'm on the top of the world. My financial situation is great, and my personal life couldn't be better. But I'm anxious and nervous and at times totally consumed by doubts and fears. I begin to question my success and find it difficult to enjoy what I have. Sometimes I feel as if it will all be gone in the morning, and I'll have to go back to my old life.

F EELING WORSE AND WORSE as things get better and better is the result of one or more of the following: (1) You feel that you have gotten to where you are, and have what you have, through circumstance and luck, not through your own effort and hard work. Since you feel that you had little to do with acquiring your status, you feel at the mercy of the "universe" or of others to maintain it. This creates great anxiety, and the fear of losing what you have clouds your enjoyment. The thought of going back to "how things were" devastates you. (2) After reaching your goal you feel you have nothing more to strive for. It was working toward your objective that gave you the greatest joy and satisfaction. You were always moving from one thing to another. Suddenly, you're no longer in pursuit of a goal, a dream. You have what you want, and you don't know how to enjoy it because your entire life was spent moving and pursuing. (3) Your anxiety may be brought on unconsciously to neutralize your elation because you feel guilty for, and undeserving of, your success. A typical thought is, *With millions of people starving, why should I be the one who has so much?* You may even create horrible images of death and destruction of your family or your possessions. When things are going too well, these thoughts are generated to punish yourself. You are not comfortable with the idea that your life is wonderful, so you generate the necessary thoughts, feelings, and emotions to bring balance—the state you feel most comfortable living in.

You have a defeatist mentality that creates a lose-lose disposition, despite the actual situation. When things are going poorly, you feel that they will get worse. When things are going well, you can't enjoy them because you're filled with anxiety waiting for the other shoe to drop.

Create a personal history. To prove to yourself how much you have contributed to your own success (almost no one succeeds by luck alone), make a time line of your life. Start with where you are today and work backward, noting all of the steps you took along the way to get you where you are. Even if you just "happened" to be in the right place at the right time, take credit for having made a sound decision to be there that day. Take your time in creating this time line; work on it every other day for at least one week.

Set new goals. The letdown you might feel after achieving a huge goal is completely natural if you haven't set yourself a new target. The best practice is to set new goals as soon as your old ones are within your grasp. Ask, "What's next for me? Once I have achieved my current goal, how will my position be improved for achieving something even greater?"

3 **Recognize how your success helps others.** Take some time to reflect on the people you have helped already and the people you will help in the future by having created your own success. If you employ other people, if you provide a service, if you sell a product that makes people's lives more enjoyable, comfortable, interesting, luxurious—if you do anything that benefits another human being—you are to be congratulated. Take pride in your contributions and consider how you can expand them. Focus on enhancing the relationships you've built and improving on what is no doubt already a valuable gift.

58

WHY DON'T I DO THE THINGS THAT I KNOW WOULD MAKE ME HAPPY?

I know what it would take to make me happy. It's not terribly hard to get or to do, and it doesn't cost very much, if anything. But I don't go for it. "It's not worth it" or "I'll do it later" are the phrases that keep bouncing around in my head while I continue to deny myself even the simplest pleasures in life. I reject opportunities and would rather help other people than selfishly "indulge" myself.

M OST OF US TRY to pamper ourselves after a long, hard day. We take the time for a hot bath, a quick nap, or a nice meal. You refuse to do the simple things that would make you happy. Why don't you take time out for yourself? The following are explanations for this behavior. (1) You feel that you deserve to relax, yet you feel guilty over actually relaxing. You feel that there is something more important and more productive that you should be doing instead. You consider unwinding and relaxing as wasting time rather than a necessary process to recharge yourself. Feeling guilty for something you did or didn't do also causes you to renounce these pleasures. (2) You have gotten comfortable being unhappy. Essentially, being happy or doing things to make yourself happy is not the governing

TIME TO GET BETTER

criterion. Being comfortable is. Put simply, you are just not comfortable enjoying yourself. You have become dependent on feeling down; in sadness you find comfort—thriving on self-pity and despair. Doing things to lift your spirits would, in effect, be counterproductive and uncomfortable. You are more comfortable being uncomfortable than being happy. (3) It's easier to rationalize old behaviors than it is to change to new ones. To justify your previous actions, you need only to continue doing what you've been doing.

While most people give themselves little incentives to motivate their behavior, you do not. Allowing yourself dessert after dinner because you jogged five miles that day is a healthy and acceptable behavior. Denying yourself a pleasure that can only be a benefit and bring joy is not. For example, "I won't take a relaxing bath because I didn't perform well on my last assignment," is a form of self-punishment. There is no benefit to denying yourself the bath.

1 **Schedule time for yourself and make this one of your "chores."** Reposition taking care of yourself as a necessity rather than a luxury. Would you expect your race car to win the Indy 500 if you never gave it a tune-up or gas? By the same token, you can't expect to perform at your maximum if you never take the time to "refuel." In addition, if you don't make the time to nurture yourself, you can begin to feel sorry for yourself. But you have no one else to blame! There is simply *no excuse* for not making your own self feel cherished.

2 **Stop rationalizing and take action!** If you already recognize the value of seeking your own happiness but haven't yet taken complete charge of this aspect of your life, then all you must do is make a decision, then set it up. If you've been putting off exercise, don't wait for the perfect opportunity to get started—start now. Find a gym and get to work. If you've been wanting to change jobs, start looking for a new one today. If you've been neglecting your vacation time, use some of it as soon as possible (not when it's "convenient" for everyone else, but when you can reasonably schedule the time). Don't wait more than a month.

There is a difference between waiting until you have the time and making the time. If you wait until free time magically appears, you may be waiting a very long time.

3   **Indulge yourself.** If there's something that you can do that would make you happy, do it. As long as it doesn't hurt you or someone else, there's no reason not to. When we die I suspect we might be called on to account for all the things we could have enjoyed in life but did not. You should treat yourself as you would your best friend. Would you ever deny your friend something that would make him or her happy?

59 WHY DO I FEEL THAT IF I GET ANYTHING OF VALUE, IT WILL BE TAKEN AWAY FROM ME?

I'm excited about a new possession, but somewhere deep down inside I have a nagging feeling that it will be taken away from me. Although I'm enjoying my new relationship, I feel that it's inevitable that my partner will leave me. I constantly worry that my life as I know it might turn upside down at any time and all the things I love will be gone.

Y OU HAVE A FUNDAMENTAL INSECURITY about the future, which stems from an insecurity about yourself. Because of your own insecurity, you feel unable to meet any challenges necessary to preserve the status of your life and the things in it. Because you take little credit for your achievements, you assume little of the responsibility in maintaining your life. Outside forces, luck, and circumstance may swipe them from you at any moment.

You may believe that you don't deserve what you have, and it will soon go to where it belongs or to someone who really deserves it. Often this is a manifestation of an experience in childhood or even in adult life, where the object of your affection—person, place, or thing—was taken away before you were ready to let it go.

This irrational fear of loss produces a myriad of consistent beliefs to foster inaction. (1) By resigning yourself to the notion that anything you get is bound to leave you, then you can do little and not feel guilty. (2) You rarely start any new business or act on new ideas because, if it's such a good idea, why didn't anyone think of it before you? (3) If you do have a good idea, somebody smarter and wealthier will steal it from you. So there's really no point in doing it. Since you fear losing what you've acquired, you may go after only what is easily obtainable. As you see it, there's no point in working hard for something if you're going to lose it anyway.

The greatest tragedy in all of this is that you develop a fundamental fear of pleasure. In your mind, happiness leads only to eventual sorrow. Since you want to avoid the pain of having pleasure stripped away from you, you rarely pursue things that will really make you happy and live in fear of losing what you do have.

1 **Enjoy what you have right now.** There are no guarantees except those Benjamin Franklin reminded us of—death and taxes. Feelings that you will be stripped of what you value come courtesy of low self-esteem. The better you feel about yourself, the less you'll worry about not being able to protect what you have. While you may lose what you gain, you will never derive pleasure from something that you don't have. As Tennyson wrote, " 'Tis better to have loved and lost than never to have loved at all."

Become aware of what you have in your life that gives you joy and happiness today and stop fearing for tomorrow.

2 **Share your wealth—what you freely give cannot be taken away from you.** Don't hoard your happiness or whatever makes you happy. Donate some portion of your time, your money, or your belongings to someone who can benefit. This can mean anything from working in a halfway house serving meals to giving old clothes to a thrift store to setting up a scholarship for neighborhood kids. Get creative! This is called *abundance thinking*; it means believing that there is enough for everyone. How can you help spread the wealth?

60

WHY DO I WORRY ABOUT THINGS THAT WILL NEVER HAPPEN OR THAT I HAVE NO CONTROL OVER?

I can spend hours thinking about earthquakes, plane crashes, nuclear war, or the sun burning out. I try to imagine what my life would be like after a nuclear war, and I would actually feel more comfortable if I had an escape bunker shielded with lead.

Y OU MAINTAIN THESE BELIEFS and logically bare irrational thoughts to comfort your inaction. "Why should I go on a diet if the world may end tomorrow?" "How can I worry about cleaning my apartment when war could break out at any moment?"

You don't feel empowered in your life and feel as if you are subject to the whims and fancies of the universe. You rarely attempt anything that even remotely depends on other people for success. You prefer to do things where you have complete control over the outcome. In this way you feel less dependent. Because you lack control of things in your life, you're not sure what in your life you do have control over. So your worry attaches itself to anything that you feel warrants your concern, whether or not you can do anything about it.

1 **Notice when you begin thinking about unlikely eventualities and redirect your focus.** The mind can think about only one thing at a time. So when your thoughts begin to turn to such irrational concerns, stop yourself as soon as you realize what you're doing. Instead, think of something you're looking forward to. What do you know will probably happen in the next few minutes? In the next hour? What are you expecting to be waiting for you when you get home tonight? What plans do you have for next week? Next month? What plans have you made in the past that have been carried out, either in recent months or as long ago as your childhood?

2 **Seek out situations where you are not the only one in control.** Just for fun, put yourself in the position of sharing power with someone else. Join a committee, take ballroom dancing, begin playing a team sport—anything where you depend on the help of others to succeed. This will help you learn the value of other people's contributions in your life. It will also help you feel that you don't have to go it alone.

61

WHY DO I DO SOMETHING HALFWAY WHEN I KNOW I'LL JUST HAVE TO DO IT OVER AGAIN?

It has to be done, and it has to be done right. I know this. But instead of doing it the right way, I cut corners just to finish it. The only problem is that it has to be redone. I could have done it right the first time, and it would have taken less time and effort than doing it over. But I just want to be done with it, albeit temporarily.

THERE ARE SEVERAL MOTIVATIONS that either individually or collectively are employed in this response. (1) You are often afraid to test your abilities by giving a job your all. A halfway job provides you an out. "Not a bad job, considering it took only ten minutes," is your constant refrain. (2) You hope that circumstances will change to make it easier to do it right at another time. You're hopeful that you'll become more motivated or inspired later. Either would make the task easier and more enjoyable to accomplish. But more often than not, your anticipated inspiration doesn't come. Those who wait to become inspired can wait a very long time. (3) It is often the case that you want a sense of satisfaction and accomplishment *now*. You don't want to wait for this sense of achievement. This mentality manifests itself in other, more common behaviors. You may eat well beyond the point that you are full. There's a sense of accomplishment in finishing the food on your plate. Leftover food translates into one more thing that you have yet to finish. (4) Your less-than-adequate performance may be the result of aggression toward others. You gain a sense of satisfaction from being unaccommodating.

When looking for something you've lost, you keep going back to the same place you've looked a hundred times before. Because you often don't do a thorough job, you don't trust yourself to have searched thoroughly for the missing item. You are willing to put in effort only when you feel good and when things are going your way. While you may want desperately to succeed, you often can't get yourself motivated. You almost never do things that are uncomfortable or uninteresting, even if there's a payoff in the end. Those who are really successful in their lives work whether they feel like it or not. You only put forth effort when things are going well.

1 If it's completion you crave, finish a small project, then get to work. Sometimes, just doing the dishes or tidying up your desk is enough. Yes, this is a form of procrastination, but it's a harmless one. Make sure you can finish this task in less than half an hour, then really go for it! And when you are ready to tackle the bigger assignment, make it right the first time. Pretend that you will never have another opportunity to make any changes once you're finished. Doing things right the first time is a habit like any other. Take all the time you need to finish the job the first time, and you will see just how productive you can be.

2 Get a mentor. Finding someone who consistently does well what you're doing halfway can be an incredible boon to your own work habits. Ask your mentor to help guide you through the process, to help you lay out an action plan. Then follow your plan to the letter.

3   **Be direct if you're angry with someone; don't indulge in passive-aggressive behavior.** Doing an incomplete job on something may temporarily derail someone else's plans, but in the long run it reflects badly on you. A more productive and healthy way to deal with disagreements is to take them directly to the person you're upset with, then be honest. Simply say, "You might be unaware that I am feeling disappointed about the way we handled that disagreement. I would like it very much if we could just clear the air." Then be sure to stay calm and try to see the other person's perspective in discussing your problem.

62 WHY AM I SO AFRAID OF AUTHORITY?

My heart races when the boss walks by. If a police officer walks over to ask me a question, I get all flustered. I'm nervous when I walk into a doctor's office, even if I'm there just to pick up a friend. I become anxious and almost disoriented when someone introduces herself as the person in charge. I feel powerless and victimized when dealing with a bureaucracy and often become frustrated to the point that I feel I can no longer deal with it.

THIS BEHAVIOR IS USUALLY the result of one or both of the following. It's likely that as a child you had a fearful experience with a person in authority. This could have been anyone from a teacher to a parent to a neighbor. Even one uncomfortable encounter could have created this negative association. It's also possible that when young you were taught to hold authority figures in unusually high esteem. This reverence for authority has stayed with you through your adult life. You don't see yourself on equal footing with others and may even feel like a child living an adult life. You are easily intimidated by authority figures and at some level feel that you have to do whatever is asked of you by someone in authority or that to question such requests is wrong. You may feel that there's so much of your world and your environment that you don't understand that you have to develop an unnatural reliance on authority.

1 **Free yourself from the limitations of the past.** In the circus, baby elephants are restrained by a strong rope or chain fixed to a post. The baby struggles against its tether but cannot break free. As the elephant grows, the animal trainer does not have to increase the strength of the rope, however, because the elephant has already determined that it can't possibly break the restraint, so he doesn't even try. A full-grown elephant can be held simply by tying a line to a chair.

Don't allow yourself to be held back by any perceived limitations in your past! What was difficult yesterday may be easy today. What was frightening could become enjoyable. What seemed impossible may be entirely within your grasp.

2 **Don't acknowledge authority that does not exist.** People in authority have power because it has been given to them. People in your life have power only if you let them. If you refuse to acknowledge someone's authority over you, then he is the one who is powerless. A shift in your perspective is all that's needed. Leverage is gained or lost in your mind first and in your world second.

Obviously, there are some people it's best to allow to *believe* they have power over you. If you refuse to cooperate with an IRS agent, you are asking for trouble. But it's empowering to know that you have a choice in every situation: You have control and power over everything that you do. No one can dictate who you are or what you make of your life at every moment.

63

WHY DO I FEEL EMOTIONALLY DRAINED EVEN WHEN THERE'S NOTHING REALLY GOING ON?

I'm not getting married in two weeks. I don't have fifteen-hour workdays, and my daily routine is far from demanding. There's nothing major going on in my life, yet I'm constantly and continually drained. I seem to expend much more energy and effort on things than other people do. Some days I can barely get myself out of bed, even when I don't have anything to do.

WITHOUT A TASK TO FOCUS ON, the mind goes on mental rampages, which can leave you thoroughly exhausted. Enthusiasm and excitement recharge your psychological batteries. Without a focused passion, your energy just gets used up. This is why when you're working really hard on a project that you're excited about, you're able to get by on much less sleep, even though you're working more. The mind needs to be focused, not scattered. Thoughts are energy, and energy that gets used and not replenished leaves you feeling very drained. Positive thoughts create positive energy, which is uplifting. Negative thoughts create negative energy, which is draining. Lack of focus leaves negative thoughts free to roam in your mind.

You also may be holding on to a lot of negative feelings. The energy required to hold on to these emotions is very draining. If this drainage continues and there is no outlet for these emotions, you are likely to become depressed. The mental energy needed for intelligent thought and functioning is all used up. All of your energy goes into suppressing the negativity while putting on a facade for the rest of the world.

You frequently feel as if you have a "full plate" with too much going on. But this is often a phantom plate filled with worries, fears, and anxieties. Not only is your plate not full, it's empty. And in this emptiness, your mind races to fill the gap that has been left by the inactivity. You are prone to obsessing over the details and trivialities of life. With nothing to draw your attention, seemingly inconsequential things are magnified to fill this void. It's for this reason that you probably have difficulty reading and absorbing new information.

 **If you're not ill, start a regular exercise program and be sure to eat a balanced diet.** Sometimes a lack of energy comes from not expending any. If your body has become accustomed to a sedentary lifestyle—with limited exercise and/or unhealthy eating habits—it shouldn't surprise you that your energy continues to dwindle. Like a fine automobile, when you give your body the fuel it needs and run it regularly, with the tune-ups and maintenance it needs every now and then, it will be constantly ready to take you where you want to go.

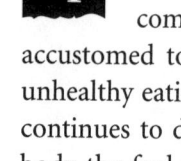 **Set a goal, something big and exciting to occupy your time and your mind.** As complex as the human mind is, it can't hold two thoughts simultaneously. When you have a passion, something to get excited about, your energy level goes though the roof. You go to bed happy and you wake up happy and excited. It doesn't work the other way around. You can't wait to get the energy and enthusiasm to pursue your goals. It won't come. You need to move in the direction that you want to go in and your desire will create its own energy.

3 **Take a quick vacation to revitalize yourself.** Often, the time when people need a vacation most is not when they've been working really hard but rather when they haven't been. But if they haven't been working at anything they feel as if they don't "deserve" a break. Forget that kind of thinking. Even two or three days away from your day-to-day life can provide the shot in the arm you need to get back on track with enthusiasm and a fresh perspective.

64 WHY DO I JUMP TO CONCLUSIONS AND READ INTO THINGS?

I see a man on the corner and build an entire life story for him. I "know" what he's doing, where he was born, how he was brought up, and if he's married. A friend tells me something, and I immediately read something entirely different into what she is saying. I often wonder what subtle glances and body posture mean and assume much more than I really should.

H UMAN BEINGS NEED A SENSE of certainty in their lives. Certainty equals security. And the less sure you are of yourself and your future, the greater your need to fill in the gaps. You may push for a resolution to situations even if it means an unfavorable result. The uncertainty is far more stressful than is a negative outcome. There needs to be a sense of completion, so if you don't have all the facts, you create them. You read into any message or situation to conform to your beliefs and thinking.

The habit of reading into what people say and do means that you rely on your own interpretation and often miss the truth around you. Instead of observing and listening to gain new information, you seek out what confirms your own thinking, ideas, and beliefs. In doing this, you miss out on the *real world* because you filter out whatever is inconsistent with your thinking and fill in the blanks to conform to your own way of thinking.

Because you have a need to know, you abhor the transitory—in essence, everything in your world. Nothing is permanent, but you need something to cling to. So you build barricades around your beliefs, ideals, and judgments, and make sure that any information coming in is consistent with your thinking. Sadly, this prevents you from seeing your reality as it actually is. This makes you increasingly insecure because you're cut off from the real world. This forces you to rely more upon your imagination to fill in the gaps.

Mysteries sell by the millions. A nail-biting suspense offers a great deal of entertainment. We love to do puzzles and games where we have a mystery to solve. You usually enjoy a little excitement as long as two criteria can be met. First, it has to end when you want it to. Being scared is no longer fun when you can't control it. It's exhilarating being on a roller coaster, but you have to believe that it is safe and that the ride will end after a few minutes. You enjoy a mystery as long as you know that you will be told the answer if you can't figure it out.

You need completion. If you're interrupted in the middle of a sentence, you need to get it out, even if you have to finish it silently to yourself.

1 **Go ahead and make assumptions, but recognize them as "fantasies" and not a reflection of reality.** It's okay to imagine things so long as you recognize that that's what you are doing. When you catch yourself jumping to a conclusion, spin another yarn that's equally compelling or amusing, then dismiss both as the mere fantasies they are.

2 **Get comfortable with being "in the dark."** Go to the movies and walk out ten minutes before it's over. (And don't ask your friends what happened!) Watch a TV show and turn it off five minutes before the end. Read a book or a magazine article and skip the last few pages or paragraphs. Don't even make up the ending for yourself; instead, just enjoy the suspense. After a week has passed, you can go back and find out the end—if you're still interested.

65 WHY AM I PREOCCUPIED WITH DEATH?

I feel uneasy even talking about it. There are times when I'm philosophical about death and think of it as a single step in one great journey. Then there are times when I'm frightened out of my mind about dying. I can spend hours on end wondering about the different ways there are to die.

A S A CULTURE we probably think about death more than we do about life. For some people this thinking keeps them from enjoying the very thing that they're so afraid of losing—life.

Any continual and constant obsession can certainly find its roots in anxiety. However, the specific nature of this preoccupation dictates that there's a more exacting foundation. Your insecurities cause you to seek permanence, but in doing so you fuel your own fears. Because you're too scared to let go of the known—which is the past—you never live completely in the unknown, which is today. You cling to the very thing that you fear the most. You cling to the past, which is dead, and hold tight to it because it offers you security, continuity, and consistency. You're generally not a big risk taker and rarely expand in any situation for fear of losing the ground you have already gained.

You look to the future as the place where you will be great. In the future you will achieve. There you will find your glory. You don't live each day complete, in itself. This is why you fear death. You have created a journey whose end can come only when you die—leaving you unfulfilled and incomplete. If you're able to die psychologically each day, then you will never again fear dying physically, because each day will be complete.

 **Know that, in a way, you "die" every day—and this is what keeps you alive.** Dead leaves fall from the tree to make way for new ones. The cells of our body regenerate; our organs, skin, and skeletons all renew themselves. Everything in nature makes way for the new by discarding the old. The only thing you cling to, the only thing that keeps you from becoming completely renewed, is your thoughts. The deadweight of the past is the only thing you carry over, each day, every day. Mental luggage weighs you down. Your fears and worries, which you carry with you from day to day, drain your vitality.

When you can live each day complete in and of itself, then there will be no fear of death. While there are obviously goals and plans that take longer than one day to finish, each day should be lived fully—and then you must let it go. In the words of Plato, "practice dying."

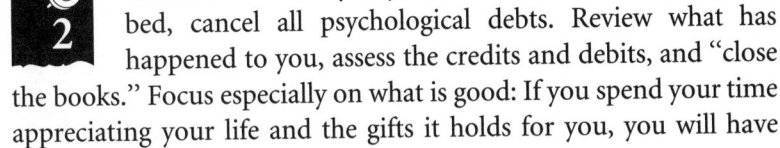 **At the end of every day, "cash in."** Just before you go to bed, cancel all psychological debts. Review what has happened to you, assess the credits and debits, and "close the books." Focus especially on what is good: If you spend your time appreciating your life and the gifts it holds for you, you will have less opportunities to dwell on death.

Enjoy each day as if it were your first, your last, and your only. Let's face it, we do have a finite amount of time here on Earth. This is all the more reason to put all our energy into *living*, not contemplating dying. The next time you find yourself drifting off into a reverie about death, stop yourself by quickly taking stock of your surroundings. Narrate your environment: "I am sitting in a comfortable chair, watching figure skating on TV. The sun is shining through the window, and my cat is sprawled on the back of my couch." Once you've brought yourself back to the present moment, ask yourself: "What is good in my life right now? What do I have that makes me feel lucky (children, spouse, home, etc.)?"

66

WHY DO I HAVE THOUGHTS OF FINDING MYSELF IN SITUATIONS WHERE I'M CONFUSED?

I have a fear of finding myself in a situation where I'm supposed to do something but don't know what it is. I have doubts that I will be able to perform what is expected of me and that my actions will cause harm to myself and to others. I feel that I may suddenly forget what I'm supposed to do at a crucial time.

YOU IMAGINE YOURSELF in situations where you have absolutely no possibility of succeeding, such as being a fighter pilot. You ask yourself, *What would I do in this situation?* Or you wonder what you would do if you suddenly had to take over someone else's position or status. These mental exercises offer you an opportunity to test yourself. Since most of your life seems unpredictable and random, these scenarios keep you in practice for unforeseen situations and events. This thinking usually stems from a lack of control in your own life. You feel that you lack the ability and confidence to control your environment and circumstance.

You often have many regrets about the way that you handled yourself in past situations. At crucial moments you feel you didn't do the right thing. You may work very badly under pressure and have a constant nagging feeling that you're forgetting something, but you're not sure what it is. You tend to do only what you know, and know well. You rarely venture outside your zone of competence because of this fear of something going wrong. It's for this reason, too, that you avoid new responsibilities and challenges.

1 **Remind yourself of what you do have control over.** Since this type of torturous daydreaming is founded on a fear of loss of control, take an inventory of all the things over which you do have control, both big and little. Make a list, from "I have control over my wardrobe" to "I can decide which route I drive to work every day"—and at the top of the list write, "I am the only one who controls my thoughts and feelings."

2 **Embark on something new.** Decide *not* to have control. In other words, control your "out-of-control" experience by choosing it for yourself. Once a day for the next week, do something completely out of the ordinary: eat lunch with a stranger, do a different type of exercise, make a phone call to a friend you haven't spoken with in years, move the pictures (or, if you're ambitious, the furniture) in your house, read the first chapter of a book you've never read.

67 WHY DO I AVOID RESPONSIBILITY?

A new job has been offered to me. It means more money, a bigger office, and more responsibility. But I decline, citing a host of explanations. Part of me wants to pursue opportunities for the better things in life, but another part hungers for the security of the way things are.

Y OU AVOID RESPONSIBILITY because you refuse to *accept* responsibility. You believe that external influences are greatly responsible for where you are and who you are today. Believing that your life is not in your own hands greatly reduces the incentive for accepting new responsibilities. Why burden yourself if the rewards of life are handed out indiscriminately?

In order to grow, in order to progress, there needs to be change. Simply, responsibility means change. But change that's for the better can still be stressful, and stress means pain. The equation now is: old comfortable situation versus the great unknown.

Accepting new responsibility usually means giving something else up. It's giving up the known that you find so difficult. You don't want to lose what you have and, more important, the comfort and security that go with it.

Whether you seek out new responsibility is essentially a question of your self-image. Responsibility brings into question your ability to handle yourself in a new situation. You would prefer to think of yourself as capable rather than risk discovering that you have faults that you aren't willing to acknowledge. To reinforce your unconscious motivation to avoid responsibility, you generalize your beliefs to limit your thinking. By adopting such beliefs as, "After thirty-five, there's no chance for marriage" or "All the good ideas have been thought of," you don't have to feel guilty for not trying.

There is also the matter of justification. It's hard for you to reconcile that all along you have had the power to make changes in your life and did nothing. If you're responsible for your life, then you need to reconcile that you may not have done all that you could have up until now. The way you've accomplished this so far is to refuse responsibility, thereby justifying your previous actions.

1 **Recognize that, regardless of what has happened in the past, whatever you do today is up to you.** There may have been many influences responsible for bringing you to where you are today—parents, teachers, friends. But your life now is in your own hands. Sink or swim, it's your show. Every action you take today reflects on what kind of person you will become tomorrow. There's no greater freedom than being responsible for your own destiny; the power you wield is enormous. You have the capacity to shape not only your future but that of others as well. **Declare the blame game over.** You can assign blame only to those who are in a position of power. And for the rest of your life, the power is yours—as is the responsibility that goes with it.

2 **Start taking some risks.** As the saying goes, ships in the harbor are safe, but that's not what ships were built for. Likewise, a person who never changes may feel comfortable, but that's not what makes us happy. What makes us happy is growing, learning, stretching ourselves as we reach for the next level. Try to view responsibility as a reward for how well you have done in the past, rather than as a burden. (People who haven't

earned some degree of respect usually aren't given responsibility.)
**Choose one area of your life where it would be great to enjoy a
greater sense of accomplishment—and take the first step by accepting responsibility in that area.**

68 WHY AM I SO EMOTIONALLY FRAGILE?

I am delicate and need to be handled with great care. If I'm not in just the right frame of mind, I'm extremely vulnerable to criticism of any kind, even when it's presented in a constructive and kind way. I can go from laughter to tears in five seconds. People always tell me that I'm just too sensitive.

Y OU HAVE AN UNDERLYING INABILITY to cope with life. You're a child in an adult's body, in an adult's life, and in an adult's world. Your emotional growth and stability have to some degree been stifled. While some people are more sensitive than others, your fragility extends beyond the scope of mere sensitivity. You have an inability to face reality, preferring to rely on images and concepts you've created to buffer your exposure to the real world.

You're overly sensitive because you exaggerate the importance of other people's opinions. It's for this reason that you have wide mood swings and need constant reassurance that you are loved and cared for. You function, in many instances, at the emotional level of a child, never wanting to grow up and face the hardships of reality.

You rarely talk about death or hardships unless you are referring to the past or to yourself. Security is the most important thing to you. You need to know that everything is okay. You don't want to hear that everything *will be okay*; you need assurance now. It's for the purpose of security that your thoughts often remain in the past. The future holds uncertainty. The past can never hurt you again and can never be altered. It's comfortable, so this is where you choose to spend your time.

You enjoy wearing your fragility on your sleeve for the world to see. You're fond of letting others know of your aches and pains and wear your disappointments like a badge of honor. Anything to show the rest of the world that you are in need of their sympathy and attention. You are lax when it comes to responsibility and often procrastinate, hoping that the task will either "just go away" or "work itself out." Like a child who covers his or her eyes with the thinking, *If I can't see you, then you can't see me*, you're of the mind-set that if you don't think about something bad, then it will not happen. You don't ask too many questions for fear that the answer will cause you stress. You just want everything to be taken care of, as you are a very needy person.

Because of your vulnerability, you are quick to read into remarks and comments by others. You can't have any unanswered worries or concerns, so all the gaps are filled in by you. You're quick to jump to conclusions, and in doing so you may very often misunderstand entire conversations. Facing reality and the ghosts that haunt the attic of your mind is the best way to defuse their power. But denying that painful aspects exist just causes them to grip harder.

 **Make a list of every single aspect of your life that you have concerns about.** Write it all down, from the death of your cat to losing your job. Writing them down does two wonderful things. First it gets them out of your head so you can look at them clearly and more objectively. Second, they don't seem so ominous when they're on paper in front of you. By writing them you acknowledge to yourself that you accept them as part of your life. Maintain this list, adding and deleting items as necessary.

Keeping this list helps you to see these as real concerns, not phantoms haunting you and ready to spring on you at any moment. You can choose when you take a look at the list, when *you* want to.

2 **Create an affirmation for yourself.** First, write a statement of how you feel about yourself in terms of how others see you. For example, "It's important for me to be approved of by other people." Then write the antidote—not an opposite, but a statement of how someone who had a healthy attitude about the opinions of others would view himself or herself. One antidote for the above statement is, "Other people's opinions of me are not as important as my opinion of myself." When you get the right one, you may think it's silly at first; that's because you don't believe it. At the same time, you'll know when you've got it. Put this statement in a place where you can't avoid looking at it at least three times a day. When you see it, read it aloud to reinforce it and empower you to believe it.

69 WHY AM I SUCH A LONER?

I've almost completely shut myself off from others. I've convinced myself that I like this lifestyle of isolation and independence, but I'm not so sure that I really do. I look down on people who are part of groups, and I feel superior to these poor joiners who need to be part of organizations. I have a resistance to engaging in and developing meaningful relationships.

O F COURSE HAVING A SENSE OF independence is a great thing. However, the reason you choose to be by yourself makes all the difference. If you prefer a lifestyle of independence and solitude because you enjoy your own company, then that's healthy and normal. If the reason for extended isolation and separatism is a dislike of others, then you may not be so well adjusted.

It is likely that you don't relate well to others. You lack interpersonal skills, and that makes it difficult for you to establish positive relationships in your personal and business lives. In more extreme circumstances you feel that the rest of the world is out to get you. You're unable to come to terms with your own inadequacies so you reconcile your lack of progress by holding the belief that the world is keeping you from succeeding. Society is to blame; you are a helpless pawn in a game that you cannot win.

If your self-imposed isolation is internally directed, you separate yourself as a means of reducing your anxiety to the exposure. Your level of discomfort causes you to retreat to your own world. You justify your behavior by taking on an air of superiority in which the rest of the world is beneath your intellect.

1   **Work at improving your communication skills.** Pick up a copy of the classic *How to Win Friends and Influence People* by Dale Carnegie, an excellent resource for building people skills. Communication skills come naturally to some people, but most of us have to learn them—and they can be mastered only if you're willing to invest the time.

2   **Remember that the surest way to get people interested in you is to become interested in them.** Interpersonal skills are something that we work on all our lives. Getting along with others and making friends can sometimes be a difficult process. Becoming comfortable with yourself is the only real way for other people to become comfortable with you. People who are secure in themselves just seem to attract a crowd. Whether you're talking to groups or individuals, when you express genuine caring about them, they generally respond positively and want to include you. So start by learning to ask questions: "What is it about skiing that you love so much?" "How did you become so involved in writing children's books?" "Have you always lived on the seashore?" For now, you don't have to join; just express an interest.

70 WHY DO I WISH I WERE SICK OR INJURED?

I silently wish from time to time that I was afflicted with an illness or sickness. I have images of myself becoming incapable of performing my job or even managing on a day-to-day basis. I wonder about how different my life would be and how differently people would treat me if I were ill.

B EYOND THE OBVIOUS EXPLANATIONS of wanting the attention, love, and concern of others, a much more prevalent factor often contributes to this response. Essentially, illness provides an excuse for not being more productive and offers an explanation that others can readily understand and accept. You're unable to motivate yourself to do more in your life, and being physically sick and unable to live a challenging life alleviates this self-imposed guilt. You want a note from your doctor excusing you from fully participating in life. You need an excuse for not doing what you feel you should, so that you can justify your inaction to yourself and to others. You need a reason for not living up to other people's expectations, so you change your circumstance. In this way, others change their expectations of you. Pretty clever.

Then comes the benefit of the next phase. Your recovery is based on your own efforts with no need for the talent, luck, or contacts that are often required in the real world. Illness changes the definition of success. Instead of becoming a millionaire, all you have to do is get better—whether by walking again, feeding yourself, sitting up in bed, whatever. You become successful and gain the respect of others under an entirely different set of rules. In this arena you don't have to rely on any external factors. It's entirely up to you. You can now move at your own pace, and your progress is not measured against anyone else's. You can become successful and enjoy the accolades and praise. All this is achieved within the scope of a new reality, dismissing the outside world and external influences. Here, anything you do is great, "considering . . ."

 **Accept what you're doing today as "good enough" for today.** As Art Williams said, "All you can do is all you can do. And all you can do is enough." If you think that you should be doing more or be more, first ask yourself what you really want. Is it possible that you're already there?

On a small island in the Caribbean, a man walking along the pier came upon a fisherman. After exchanging pleasantries the man asked the fisherman what his goals were for the future. "Well," he said, "I'm going to work a little longer each day to catch extra fish. This fish I will sell at the market. Then when I have enough money saved I'm going to buy a small boat so I can go out into deeper waters and catch even more fish. Soon I will have enough money for a second boat, which my son will use. Then we will have many boats and I will no longer need to work." "What will you do once you retire," asked the man. The fisherman thought for a while and then said, "Well, I suppose I'll spend my days fishing."

If you're preoccupied by the idea of becoming ill, beware. Science is continually discovering more and more evidence for the profound link between mind and body, between thoughts and physical reality. If you don't make yourself seriously ill, you could at least develop a psychosomatic illness. This fascination with being sick can sometimes be the first step on the road to becoming a hypochondriac. Guard against this possibility by getting realistic about what an illness could cost you: your energy and enthusiasm, your independence, your livelihood, even your life. To really bring the point home, volunteer some time at a local rehabilitation center or hospital. You'll recognize very quickly that while the people who are fighting an illness may be admirable and courageous, you do them a disservice by wishing to put yourself in their shoes simply as a self-indulgence or to gain pity.

71 WHY DO I FEEL AS IF I'VE GOT THE ABSOLUTE WORST LUCK?

I'm always picking the slowest line at the supermarket. The person in front of me takes the last good parking spot. The woman with the high hair always sits in front of me at the movie theater. Out of a group of ten people, I'm the only one who gets splashed by the moving car. I feel that I can't get a decent break in life and that the tide is always against me.

LIFE HAS DEALT YOU A BAD HAND. You could do and be so much more if you weren't at such a disadvantage. If this thinking sounds familiar, you're probably confusing bad management with destiny. This thinking provides an effective and comforting rationalization for not being everything that you know you can be. It takes the responsibility for your life out of your hands and takes away the pressure of having to contend on an equal footing.

There's a discrepancy between what life has given you and what you feel you should have gotten. Since the fragility of your own ego prevents you from accepting the responsibility, the rest of the world must be to blame. In placing the blame for your circumstance on external factors, you are able to reconcile the discrepancy. As a way to make right these injustices, you indulge yourself whenever an opportunity presents itself. Your happiness is your own responsibility, and you seek out opportunities that promote this gratification, whatever the cost.

 **Alter your perceptions of your world.** Are you *always* in the slowest line—or just sometimes? Do you *never* get a good seat in a theater—or is it that you notice only when you're behind someone with big hair?

Start paying better attention and make special notice whenever anything goes *right*. If you're going to attribute everything to "luck," then go all the way. What great luck I'm having that my car started this morning! How lucky I am that the weather is good today! I'm so lucky to live in a place with clean air!

Sooner or later, you're bound to start feeling more lucky—or to give up the belief that what happens to you always has to do with *your* good or bad luck.

Expect to have good things happen to you. Is there such a thing as having "bad luck"? Actually there is, sort of. You have bad luck because, in effect, you expect it. Just as the ozone filters out the sun's harmful rays, whatever you experience in the world gets filtered through your expectations.

How often have you noticed the occurrence of streaks? Don't things seem to happen in a pattern? When you're on a roll, you're on a roll; and when you're not, you're not. Some days nothing can go wrong; then there are the days that you wish you never got out of bed.

Your expectations play a powerful role in how your reality unfolds. You get what you expect. Life is not difficult; people make it difficult for themselves. It can be unfair and at times cruel, but this doesn't mean you should expect the worst at every turn. If you do that, you will find life to be incredibly painful. If you can shake this habit and start expecting the best life has to offer, great things will surely start happening to you.

Interpret situations positively whenever possible. Not only does reality conform to your expectations, but the very same event can be interpreted very differently. If you're convinced that you're having a great day, a car that comes within inches of hitting you will be greeted with a feeling of good fortune: *Wow, was I lucky.* If you just "know" that you're going to have a bad day, then that same near miss will be greeted with, *I almost got killed. Nothing ever goes right for me.* Same event. One way of thinking puts you in a great mood, the other way makes you even more miserable. Tell yourself every morning and throughout the day that you are having a great day and that everything's going your way. You may be surprised at just how great your day will be.

72 WHY DO I FEEL LIKE I'M "FOOLING" THE WORLD?

I'm on top of my game; I've got it all, and more. However, I'm wondering when someone will "discover" me. I feel I will soon be "found out." I often question if I'm truly worthy of my accomplishments and achievements. I wonder if I really deserve to be where I am. I feel I'm getting away with something, like I'm fooling everybody.

F EELING LIKE YOU will soon be "discovered" is indicative of feelings of inadequacy. Although you have accomplished much, you feel that anyone could have done it and that you just got lucky. You have no appreciation for any special talent or ability you have because you don't internalize your success. Because you feel unworthy, you are not able to acknowledge the correlation between your effort and the result it produces. You attribute your success to external circumstances such as timing or luck.

You question if you will be able to keep up the pace of your success. There's the feeling that it's all a charade. Someday someone is going to take it from you and give your success to someone who is more deserving. You don't believe that people are seeing the real you, and you are waiting to be exposed for "who you really are."

1 **Get clear about who "the real you" is.** Getting to know oneself is a worthy, lifelong pursuit. To take your understanding to a deeper level, write a description of yourself as you think the world sees you, then write a description of who you think the "real you" is. Consider where the discrepancies lie. Is there anything really great about you of which most people are unaware? If there is, you don't need to be afraid of these "secrets" getting out! Are your so-called flaws anything that other people wouldn't understand or relate to? What could you do today to start improving in the areas that you think might be embarrassing?

2 **Start broadcasting your real self to the world.** You can't be "found out" if you are completely honest with people. This is not to say that you must retell your life story to everyone you meet, but you must give up trying to impress people with exaggerations. And if luck played a role in getting you where you are today, acknowledge it. The fact is, if you arrived at your current level of success purely by luck, most people would simply admire your luck, not begrudge your achievements.

73 WHY DO I TALK TO MYSELF?

I'm not able to shut myself off. My mind is always going, twenty-four hours a day, seven days a week. I'm not able to clear my mind and mentally unwind.

WE ALL TALK TO OURSELVES—this is normal. However, if you're not able to shut yourself up, then this is indicative of the following: You don't know how to shut your thoughts off. You have become a mental addict. Your mind is constantly working, chattering. It never rests. There is a vast difference between thinking of nothing and not thinking. The former requires effort, while the latter does not. A mind that is constantly churning is a mind that cannot rest. This continuous flow can turn into a flood that can be overwhelming. A nervous breakdown can occur as a means of shutting off the stream of thoughts. A breakdown is really an overload of thoughts. The expression, "You've gone out of your mind," is an accurate description of what is happening. It's the only way to escape from the barrage of thoughts.

If the clutter in your mind becomes intolerable, you may resort to talking out loud to yourself. With a mind full of random and often unwelcome thoughts, at times you can't "hear yourself think." You need then to think out loud in order to separate those thoughts that you want to pay attention to from those you do not. Since you cannot filter out unwanted thoughts, you separate them by voice.

The clutter of your mind is often reflected in your surroundings. The person with a cluttered mind often has a cluttered office and a cluttered home. Your way of thinking is almost always reflected in your way of life.

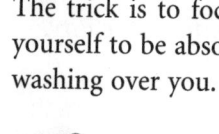 **Take up meditation or yoga.** Studies suggest that people who talk to themselves are actually smarter than folks who don't, so you probably need to worry only if you start to answer yourself. However, meditation and relaxation techniques such as yoga can be a wonderful tool to help you gain the ability to quiet your mind, to create a time of stillness and serenity that can brace you throughout the day.

Listen to music. If you just want a quick mental break, play music loudly. For some people, music with lyrics does it, and for others strictly instrumental is just as effective. The trick is to focus completely on what you're hearing, to allow yourself to be absorbed by the sounds and the feelings of the music washing over you.

Do something that requires a lot of physical effort. Invigorating exercise is a great stress reliever and a way of turning off that incessant internal chatter. Take up a sport or activity such as jogging, bicycling, swimming, or racquetball. You'll find that your mind either directs all its focus toward the task at hand (such as returning your opponent's serves and shots across the tennis net) or occupies itself peacefully (as in long-distance running). What a difference it makes!

Organize your life. Have you ever noticed that when you are away on vacation your mind feels clear and calm? Of course this is because you're away from it all. But away from what? You're not surrounded by clutter and disarray. This is why we're often in a better mood when we've cleaned up our office or home. You can simply think more clearly and calmly.

74

WHY DO I SPEND A LOT OF TIME FANTASIZING AND DAYDREAMING?

While other people may daydream when they're bored, I spend much of my time living in a world created by my imagination. I reinvent the past and think about how differently things might have turned out if only . . . I can daydream for hours about my future but do little in the way of making my fantasy a reality.

YOU SPEND YOUR TIME in a fantasyland because it's far more enjoyable than your own reality. While many successful people have been dreamers, there is a marked distinction between them and what you're doing. Those who dream and plan and then put their plans into action are much different from those who conjure up images of wealth and success and then do nothing to work toward them. You set unrealistic goals and have expectations far beyond your grasp. Because you are unhappy with where you are in life, you rely on your dreams of a better tomorrow to lift your mood. By creating entire scenarios of wealth and romance, you escape your own reality.

Your imagination often takes you to the past. You fantasize about what you would have done differently and how things might have worked out if only . . . You reinvent the past because it's comforting. You can be and achieve whatever you want in it. Instead of clear-cut goals and plans, you look to some faraway point in your life and say, "That is where I want to be." Inventing the future is your alternative to living in the present.

You're not able to accept your limitations, so you invent another existence in your imagination. In extreme instances, your fantasies take the place of achievement in the real world. If your own world were interesting and exciting, then there would be no reason to escape from it. When your imagination doesn't carry you far enough away, you may turn to drugs to enhance it, food and alcohol to dull it, and in extreme cases suicide to leave it.

1 **Create a plan for realizing your favorite daydream.** Daydreaming is fine as long as it doesn't serve as a substitute for achievement. When your thoughts turn to unrealistic fantasies, think of an attainable goal that you would like to accomplish. Your own life can hold magnificent accomplishments.

Which of your daydreams could become a reality if you set your mind to it? Create a plan by working backward from the goal and determining what you must do days before you achieve it, a month before, two months, three months, and so on, until you've worked your way back to today. When you know what you must do to start moving toward this goal now, take action! Take your first step today, then follow through tomorrow, and the next day, and the next, until you've reached your goal.

2 **Live in the present.** You will be spending the rest of your life in the future, so spend only as much time thinking about the past as you spend living in it—in other words, none. The future is best served by taking care of the present. If you do what you must right now, the future will take care of itself.

75 WHY DO I ROUTINELY RATIONALIZE THINGS IN MY LIFE?

I'm working on something that really needs to be done, but I decide to take a nap so I'll be more refreshed. However, when I awake, I find that tomorrow might be a better day to begin. I write down a "to do" list for the next day, filling it ambitiously with many tasks and goals. The next day comes, and I'm lucky if I get to one of them.

L IE TO MYSELF? What? Why? You may live most of your life lying to yourself and rarely, if ever, are you completely honest. You probably don't even have an accurate picture of how many times you are less than completely honest with yourself. Without ever realizing it you are constantly changing your ideas, goals, and plans to accommodate your thinking. You probably have no idea how much of your life you rationalize away. You don't permit yourself to see the world and your life as they really are. From the diet you'll start on Monday to the assignment you'll work on all next week, you convince yourself that *this time* will be different. But it never is.

You would rather succeed in your mind than risk failing in the real world. You refuse to acknowledge your life as it exists and project your thoughts to a place where you prefer to live—the future. In the future, everything will be different, or so your thinking goes.

Always living in the future means that your life is wasted in the present.

Why do you lie to yourself? If you didn't lie to yourself, then you would have to look at some very painful aspects of yourself and of your life that you may not be prepared to accept. In the end, you may end up rationalizing away your entire life. Everything with you is always, "I'm too tired," "It's not worth it," "It really doesn't matter." You're always waiting for the perfect time, but that time never comes.

Much of your time and energy has been diverted in the wrong direction. You tell yourself how wonderful you are, and you list your attributes and qualities. To see yourself as you truly are, you must see all your negative attributes as well as positive, see who and what you have become. But you just want to look at the good qualities. This only furthers the covering of the negative and hastens your need to hide from them.

When you lie to yourself, you're really trying to hide from yourself. But refusing to see what is doesn't make it go away. Have you ever refused to accept that your new car may be leaking oil? Or have you told yourself, in spite of overwhelming evidence to the contrary, that your partner is not cheating on you?

There's the old joke about a man looking for a lost quarter under the streetlight. When a passerby asks where he dropped the quarter, the man points to a dark area at some distance. The passerby asks curiously, "If you dropped the quarter over there, why are you looking for it here?" The man simply responds, "Because the light's better." Like this man, we often fool ourselves into wasting time and energy because we don't want to face certain hardships of our reality.

Here's a good yardstick to measure this behavior. If you continue to do the same things and expect different results, it's time to review your thinking. A simple fact of life is that nothing changes unless you do. If you want things to be different, you need to change what you've been doing. Rationalizing is probably the greatest single cause of inaction. And the smarter you are, the more clever the lie. But in the end the only one who gets hurt is you. See, and take action—don't run and hide.

 **The next time you start coming up with an excuse for not following through, for not moving forward, or for any behavior,** *stop.* Remind yourself, "I don't pay the price for success—I pay the price for failure." Tack this phrase up in a room where you spend most of your day and refer to it whenever you feel a rationalization coming on.

 **Once you stop yourself from making an excuse, do what you know you should.** Taking responsibility for your own actions is a learned response, and it will grow stronger with practice. Every time you give up an excuse and just go for it, you create one more link in a strong, positive chain of action. However, if you're going to do something that you know is stupid, admit that. You're better off acknowledging that it's a bad idea than doing it and convincing yourself that it makes sense. Do not lie to yourself. Other people will be more than happy to fulfill this obligation.

76

WHY IS IT SO HARD FOR ME TO STOP DESTRUCTIVE HABITS?

Smoking, drinking, shopping, whatever the habit, whether harmless or hazardous, I just can't break it. Other people seem to have so much more willpower than I do. I can't even break habits that I no longer enjoy.

ARE THESE THINGS HABITS just because you've done them for so long, or is there something else? Are habits harder for you to break than they are for other people? Why can some people just stop cold turkey, while you wrestle for years with a habit?

It's not the time associated with the habit per se, but the lack of awareness. The longer you engage in a behavior, the more unaware you become of the actual activity. The only difference between a habit and an action is the level of awareness you give to the behavior. A habit is a dead process, it's automatic. Focusing on your habit breathes life into it so that it is no longer mechanical. In this way you can stop it.

Your difficulty in breaking away lies in your inability to focus your attention. If you put your hand on a hot stove, you would remove it because it was painful. If you were unconscious, your lack of awareness would not cause you to take this action.

You are unaware of the process of your behavior; you only move through the motions. It's a purely mechanical process. Those people who are able to alter their behavior and change long-term habits are able to pay attention to the process. This is why those who are nervous and high-strung are more apt to have negative habits and to have a harder time breaking them. It's their inability to focus their attention that prevents them from easily breaking away from the mechanical process. Stress and anxiety clutter your ability to focus.

It's particularly hard for you to break away from habits if you feel that you are not fully in control of your life. You won't feel that you have control in your life if you don't have control over the things in your life. Giving up a habit like smoking is perceived as giving up control over one more thing. Going on a diet is internalized as giving up control of your eating to a diet regimen. You need to hold on to these things because they are the only things in your life you feel you can control.

 **Record your activities.** To help you create awareness of your habit, and to reward yourself when you don't indulge in it, for one month dictate your every move into a portable tape recorder. Your entries would sound something like this: "6:15 A.M. Got up, took a shower, and got dressed. 6:45 Ate breakfast (toast and coffee) and read the paper. 6:55 Drove to work. 7:30 Arrived at work, had Danish. 8 Meeting with sales team." Transcribe your tape once a week. If this person were dieting, she would highlight the food areas and just become aware of what was being eaten and when. And the next time she was offered something that was not on her diet, she'd think twice about taking it because it would become "real" the minute she had to speak it into her recorder.

Things like willpower and motivation are often ineffective because the full impact of the behavior falls outside your field of awareness. This exercise helps break down the automation cycle and revitalize the behavior.

When you do this, be sure also to include any time you had the urge to indulge in the behavior you're trying to change *and exercised restraint.* Circle these on your transcript and give yourself a pat on the back!

2 **Create a "punishment and reward" system based on your transcript.** For example, whenever you have more than two items highlighted per day for the week, "punish" yourself by scrubbing the toilet or doing some other chore you don't enjoy, and whenever you have more than five circles per day, give yourself a reward of some sort.

77 WHY DO I UNDERMINE MY OWN EFFORTS?

I feel as if I'm not always on my own side, as if two personalities are inside me. There's a force within that holds me back, like the reins of a horse. Part of me wants to succeed, and part of me hopes that I fail. My life is like a car driven with one foot on the accelerator and another on the brake. I use up a lot of energy, but I don't seem to go very far.

YOU WANT IT, and you may be willing to do whatever it takes to get it, but you aren't able to. Why not? First, *ability* does not mean *mobility*. The fact that you're able to do something and want to do it does not necessarily ensure that you will. The challenge is that you are not willing to risk injury to your self-image by taking actions to bolster and expand it. You are afraid to put your ability to the test. You're not willing to risk giving up what you are to chance becoming something greater.

Your self-concept shapes your thoughts and behavior and ultimately your destiny. How you see yourself and the world determines how you move through it. Fear protects the ego. Just as you go to great lengths to protect yourself from physical harm, so too do you protect your psychological self. If you think for a moment of all the things you would like to do but don't, you can trace the root of your resistance to your ego and the protection of it.

Let's say you want to go on a diet to lose fifty pounds. You can absorb every bit of knowledge on the subject and be willing to do whatever it takes to be successful and still not succeed. First you have to overcome the habits of rationalizing, such as, "I'm happy the way I am," "The timing isn't right," "Maybe I just don't have the will-power and discipline that other people seem to have." Next you have to contend with a fierce inner battle. If you are successful, will you feel you deserve to be? Will you be able to handle it, or will you feel too uncomfortable? Will you feel uncomfortable with the success or even with the change itself? Will your success affect or upset anybody else? What if the desired results are achieved and you are still not happy? And what if you aren't successful? All that time wasted. What will others think of your failure? Will you be mad at yourself? Will others be mad at you?

You need successes in life to bolster your self-image so you can meet with failure and not be devastated. But the only way to expand your self-image often entails putting your image at risk of injury. You're rarely willing to risk injury because your self-image is too fragile. So you remain fearful of growth and disguise your inaction with lies wrapped in rationalizations. While part of you desperately wants to succeed, another part remains fearful of losing what you've already gained. The fragility of your ego cannot withstand any further assault. Conversely, someone who feels great about himself or herself is eager for new risks and challenges and has an ever-expanding self-image.

Childhood is where our self-concept is initially molded and formed. The opinion you hold of yourself today greatly reflects the influences of yesterday. It's likely that your influences were less than positive, and your subsequent actions began to express these beliefs about yourself. This sets in motion a network of habits, thoughts, and beliefs that remains consistent with a low self-image.

Additionally, your values and goals in life need to be consistent with one another. We all have fears and we all have desires. When one conflicts with the other, they pull you in two different directions.

For example, the goal to lose fifty pounds and the fear of intimacy may conflict if you feel that becoming more attractive will put you closer to finding a romantic interest. When you set your goals, make sure that your fears do not hinder your efforts.

1   **Confront your fears.** The root of all irrational fear can be traced to a fear of self-discovery. It's often an aspect of yourself that you're unwilling to confront or expose. Ask yourself what you are afraid will happen if you achieve this goal. If you can't think of anything, ask if there is anything you can *imagine* being frightened of when you achieve this goal. Simply writing the fears on paper is often enough to help you see how irrational they are and how unlikely they are to be realized.

2   **Review the influences of your past on your current opinion of yourself.** Who was important in helping to create your self-image? How many of these people positively influenced you? How many negatively? Examine each of their contributions and assess whether they empowered or demoralized you. Visualize throwing the "demoralizing" ideas into a great composting pile and planting the "empowering" ones in a lovely garden. Imagine that later that week you will go back to the compost heap and find that your old garbage has been transformed into valuable fertilizer that will make your empowering self-concept grow and flourish. Repeat this visualization every day, twice a day, for two weeks.

78 WHY DO I FEEL UNIMPORTANT?

I feel my life has very little meaning and that my accomplishments are few and inconsequential. I feel the world will go along quite nicely with or without me, and I sometimes feel that others would be better off if I were not around. In periods of reflection I know that my ideas, dreams, and hopes will never be realized. I feel that others aren't very interested in me as a person and often don't take me very seriously.

E VER SINCE WE WERE LITTLE we have been taught that our value comes from what we can do. From the finger painting that gets put on the refrigerator door to the bonus at work, the source of our pride has always been external, when it should be internal. What happens when you are no longer producing and have no other source of self-appreciation and pride?

You feel that you have to *do* something in order to *be* someone. The sadness in this truth is found in the following. Someone asks you who you are, and you respond by saying you are a doctor, an Indian chief, a secretary, whatever. This person didn't ask you what you *do*. You confuse *who you are with what you do*. There is the feeling that unless you make a tangible contribution all of the time, you are unimportant. This is why most people go after tangible results. They need to wave the banner of success and say, "Look at me, I'm somebody." Those who embark on a spiritual journey and renounce their possessions and status have little in the way of proof of their successes. This is one reason why so few do it.

You often become infuriated and enraged over being cut off on the highway. You see this as a personal attack. You feel that the other person is taking advantage of you. He does not respect you and may be out to get you. This is why you are so intent on seeing what the other driver looks like. You want to see if the driver is the *type of person* who would do this on purpose. Of course your interpretation of the type is based on your stereotype of what a jerk looks like. You get angry because your fragile ego has been challenged.

Imagine that you decided to renounce all your worldly goods. What would you then "possess" that would make you special in this world? Discuss this hypothetical situation with a good friend, your spouse, or someone else you feel close to. (This helps because for some people it's difficult at first to come up with any ideas.) Be sure to focus on the internal as well as external. In other words, discuss character traits, personality nuances, talents.

Come up with an alternative "job title." What would be an accurate answer to the question, Who are you? (Remember, "I'm a stockbroker" is an answer about what you *do*, not about who you are. A better answer would reflect the person you described above.) For example, "I am a loving, caring parent who enjoys his work as a stockbroker. I thrive on competition and love to play racquetball" is on target. Notice that the statement describes feelings and talents rather than the work that is performed.

Who you are is something very different from what you do. How you live your life is not the same as what you do to earn a living. We make a living by what we do, but we make a life by what we can give. Loving yourself and appreciating who you are is the best gift you can give to the rest of the world. Because when you love and respect yourself you can love and respect others.

79 WHY DO I DWELL ON NEGATIVE THOUGHTS?

I want to think good, happy, positive thoughts, but I end up dwelling on negative ones instead. I'm often so consumed by these negative thoughts and emotions that it is difficult for me to concentrate on anything else. My mind is constantly turning and churning to the point where I need to eat, drink, or take drugs to stop the flood of thoughts.

CONSTANT AND CONSISTENT DWELLING on negative thoughts drains you physically and mentally. At times it can leave you tired and depressed. While obsessive thinking of negative thoughts may be a symptom of and a precursor to depression, it is a symptom itself of something entirely different.

There are several "benefits" derived from this response. (1) It provides a way for you to get back at yourself. If things are going well and you begin to feel undeserving, these thoughts serve as a way to punish yourself. (2) If you feel uncomfortable with your "happiness," negative thoughts provide you with enough sadness to balance out the happiness, to a point where you feel more comfortable. (3) Lack of direction and passion often contributes to this response. If you don't have a passion or focus in your life, then you have nothing to consume your attention. Your thoughts are free to wander. Unless you make a conscious effort to think positively, your thoughts dwell on the negativity around you. (4) You may have an overwhelming need to prepare yourself psychologically for life's little surprises. You don't feel emotionally equipped to handle bad news, so you prepare yourself to reduce the shock. By dwelling on negative thoughts you feel you will be better able to deal with a negative situation than if you are in a good mood and receive bad news. This way it's less of a transition—you're already in a bad mood anyway. In this way, no one and nothing can unexpectedly take your good mood away from you. You're prone to expecting the worst for this very reason. You have a strong need to be prepared psychologically for life's bumps and shocks. Expecting the worst also eliminates potential disappointment.

 **Get in the habit of thinking positively.** We live in a negative society, surrounded by bad news from the morning paper until the evening update. In general, our culture is not charged with a positive atmosphere. Every day we make a choice to fill our minds with either positive or negative thoughts. To break out of a rut of negative thinking, you need to get in the habit of thinking positively.

Dwelling on negative thoughts is a learned behavior. And what has been learned can be unlearned. Negative thinking is like a train— it picks up speed and power the farther it moves along. You need to stop your thinking in its tracks. In time you'll find that unwanted thoughts go as easily and quickly as they come. It's just a matter of retraining your mind.

Start by creating "mental bullets" that you can fire at negative thoughts. Review in your mind several things that you're genuinely excited about. Whenever a negative thought creeps in, fire a positive one at it. Visualize the negative thought exploding like a clay duck. In time you will naturally think happy, positive thoughts without even thinking about it.

2 **Play a mental endurance game.** If you were promised $1,000,000 for every minute you could think positively, continuously, without a single negative thought creeping in, how much money do you think you could earn? The one thing we all have complete and absolute control over is our thoughts. So if you can control your thoughts and are free to think whatever you want to, why don't you think positive, happy thoughts all of the time?

80 WHY DO I EAT WHEN I'M NOT HUNGRY?

I eat when I'm hungry and I eat when I'm not. It doesn't really matter. Sometimes I try to eat fast so I can get as much food in before I feel full or nauseated. I don't always enjoy eating, and it's become so mechanical I'm barely aware of the process anymore.

PEOPLE EAT FOR A VARIETY OF REASONS other than hunger. The reasons include but are certainly not limited to depression, boredom, loneliness, to fill a void, to be self-destructive, to feel enjoyment, to insulate themselves from others, anger, chemical or energy imbalance, anxiety, guilt, fear, and on and on. There are hundreds of books on the psychological and physical causes of overeating. While the explanations and theories vary and often contradict one another, the root of this behavior is undeniably the same in all cases.

You eat when you are not hungry for one reason and one reason only: You need to dull your awareness of yourself. And that's it! You don't like the way you're feeling, the mood you are in, and the thoughts you are thinking.

You are highly vulnerable to stress, which often makes you in great need of escape. When fantasies and dreams do not provide adequate distraction, you seek drugs, alcohol, or food to distance yourself further from your thoughts. When you say that you are *under a lot of stress*, you are in fact experiencing a flow of negative thoughts that you can't turn off. So you do the only thing that you can. You attempt to dull your awareness of them.

Food is the logical choice to alter your mood for several reasons. (1) Food tastes good. It's enjoyable and satisfying. (2) The full feeling you get after eating is comforting. It allows you to "feel" something. (3) It's a physical distraction; the actual eating process requires your attention. (4) Food is legal, and it's easy to eat. (5) Food alters your body's chemistry; foods containing caffeine or sugar provide a temporary lift. (6) The gratification is immediate.

The most critical factor, though, has to do with control. If you suffer from this behavior, then you probably don't feel that you have much control over your life. You certainly don't have control over your thoughts, which means it would be difficult for you to be in complete control of your life. Since you cannot control your thoughts, you use what you can control—food—to try to dull your awareness. You become dependent on food to compensate for the lack of control you have over your thoughts. You maintain control of your mood through proxy. If you're feeling down, you don't have the ability to "snap" yourself out of it, so instead you eat a piece of cake. Additionally, this lack of control makes you even more determined to be in charge of anything in your life that you *can* control. So you'll be damned if you will let some diet tell you what you can and can't eat.

When you feel like eating something and you're not hungry, stop for just a moment. What usually happens is that you attack the food with an almost crazed passion. But if you stop just long enough to become aware of what you're doing you can halt your actions. Then you can choose any of the following options.

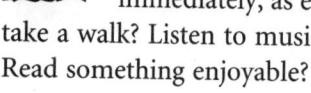

Create a list of ten enjoyable things you can do instead of eating. These should be activities that you can do immediately, as easily or more easily than eating. Can you take a walk? Listen to music? Take a hot bath or shower? Meditate? Read something enjoyable?

Post your list of ten things in your kitchen, office, or on your refrigerator door—someplace where you will see it on your way to eat. Then, when you feel the urge to stuff your face, select one of the items from your list to do instead. These choices will give you the mood alteration you are seeking without adding inches to your waist!

2 **Set a timer for ten minutes and don't eat until the time is up.** Often the impulse to eat is in response to discomfort in the moment. If you allow ten minutes to pass before you actually go for the food, you will often find that the urge to eat has either diminished or vanished. And make sure you set the timer and then put it somewhere you can't see it! You don't want to be counting the seconds until you eat; you want to give your brain a chance to focus on something other than food.

During those ten minutes, take ten deep breaths and drink a large glass of water. It could be your body isn't craving food but wants oxygen and fluids instead. Both deep breathing and drinking water can give you a physiological change of state. The water will also give your stomach the "full" feeling that most people associate with comfort.

3 **If you still feel like eating, proceed, but do so differently.** If you're using a fork, hold it in the other hand. If you're eating with your hands, mentally count the number of times that you chew your food. This makes you physically aware of your actions. As you become aware of each bite it is harder for you to eat mechanically.

4 **Move your body.** Your physiology is directly correlated to your psychological state. When people are in a negative, self-destructive mood, there is invariably a corresponding posture. This posture is usually characterized as sitting and still. Get up and move your body—your thoughts will follow. You can "jog" yourself mentally simply by moving your body. Try it.

81

WHY DON'T I DO MORE WHEN I'M CAPABLE OF SO MUCH?

I honestly and truly believe that I can do and be anything in the world that I want. I see other people far less talented than I am succeeding and enjoying the good life. It's not that I'm lazy, but something holds me back from going full steam ahead. It's become so frustrating, wanting more out of life but not going after it.

Y OU ARE DIFFERENT from someone who sabotages his or her own success due to underlying feelings of unworth. Your lack of success is not based on incompetence or low self-esteem.

It's likely that you are among the more talented people, with great abilities and talents in many areas. The challenge is that while you may have a passion pushing you in one direction, you have other interests pulling you in another. A lack of focus often leads you to dabble in many areas. You like to "try" different things but often have little to show for your short-lived effort. Without this focus, your energy and attention are scattered. Accomplishment of any magnitude is difficult without follow-through. While you can move in any direction you wish, you freeze and do nothing because you cannot narrow your passion and attention. To compound your situation you're probably prone to thinking ideas right out of existence. By this I mean that you dwell on them constantly and insatiably. So much so that after a while an idea no longer seems fresh. You've worked and reworked it so many times in your head that it no longer excites you. Then you move on to something "new."

You may feel guilty for not making full use of your natural talents and abilities. You put too much emphasis on a successful outcome, and so you are reluctant to press forth. You resign yourself to imagining how wonderful it would be if... There may also be unconscious motivations for your lack of sustained effort. If you do succeed you'll have nothing to look forward to. It's in the planning and dreaming that you derive the most pleasure.

 Choose a single objective, something you're excited about, and create a plan and a time line for achieving that objective. Make sure it's something that is achievable in a relatively short amount of time—you want to train your mind into believing that achieving what you want is pleasurable!

For this short amount of time, put all your attention into achieving your objective. Pursue it until you have gotten what you want. If you find yourself distracted, tell yourself, "I can do that later. Right now, this is what I'm working on." You can move in opposite directions, but not at the same time. You can have whatever you want in life, but you can't get it all at the same time.

 **Set aside a specific time each week to pursue something that has little or no connection to your overall objective.** It could be that your brain is craving variety, and that's why you find it difficult to focus consistently on anything. Giving yourself permission to take a "brain break" allows you to keep your attention on your main goal for the rest of the time. You may even find that something you learn in your "brain break" activity may help you achieve your bigger goals!

 **Stay connected to the passion behind your objective.** If you're not emotionally connected to why you want to attain something, it is much easier to be distracted by other, newer pursuits. Take the time to write a description of why

you're on the particular path you've chosen. Come up with as many emotional reasons and phrases as you can, words that get you excited and make your path meaningful for you. Each day, when you get up in the morning, or when you get to the office or start your work, review your objective, time line, and reasons for wanting this particular goal. Commit anew to achieving all you desire. You'll find it much easier to be a laser when you are connected emotionally to your target!

82

WHY AM I OBSESSED WITH MY APPEARANCE?

While I consider myself to be smart, friendly, and interesting, it's my appearance that I am most concerned with. I check myself out every time I walk by a mirror. I don't like anyone to see me when I'm not looking my best.

Y OU MAY BE UNDER THE IMPRESSION that *good-looking equals good person.* This belief is in part culturally induced. Every day, we see many attractive people getting better service and more attention. When you carry this thinking to an extreme, you fall outside this cultural preoccupation and into a personal obsession.

This means that you feel people won't like you unless you look good. You feel you will be treated poorly and meanly if others, even of the same sex, do not find you to be attractive. You believe that you cannot get ahead in this world unless you are physically appealing. Your appearance is your passport to success.

You feel that your appearance is your greatest, if not your only, asset. By placing such emphasis on your looks, you become obsessed with maintaining them. You may not necessarily consider yourself to be particularly attractive, but you seek to enhance what you do have, often turning to cosmetic surgery. Your own opinion of yourself is greatly influenced by how you are received and perceived by other people.

You may be characterized as one who is flirtatious. You seek feedback from others to provide confirmation of your self-concept. As you age you are prone to a middle-age crisis as your greatest asset diminishes in "value." Your thinking is in part due to how you perceive others. If you only respect someone who is wealthy or good-looking, then you believe people will only respect you if you are these things. The criterion that you use to judge others is the same one you feel they are using to judge you. If you consider personality to be the governing criterion for liking other people, then that is the main quality by which you feel others are judging you. Choosing not to judge others will greatly reduce your own obsession with your appearance.

 **Deliberately omit one item of your usual personal grooming for one day.** Wear your glasses instead of contact lenses. If you always style your hair very carefully, just run a comb through it. If you never leave the house without lipstick, leave it off for one day. If your clothing is always coordinated and accessorized perfectly, stop dressing when you consider yourself "half-done"—wearing just a shirt and pants, or no jewelry—and leave the house.

Go through your day and notice the reactions of people around you. Some may notice that you look different, but most people won't even see the change! Your appearance is only a small part of how people relate to you. More important is what you possess inside and the love and attention you give to other people.

 **Volunteer at a local shelter, hospital, or anywhere there are people in need of help.** Spend time contributing to others. As a real stretch, volunteer for something where you'll get extremely grubby—cleaning, outdoor work, etc. Watch the other volunteers around you and how people relate to each other. You'll find that the people who receive the most love aren't the best looking or most groomed or wealthiest—they are the people who give the most to others. They're not focused on how they look; they're focused on what the other person needs.

When you find yourself judging someone, catch yourself and ask, "What's great about this person?" "What could I like about him or her?" Observe that person until you find something you can like and respect, something that has nothing to do with appearance. And do the same thing with yourself! Very often, when we have the habit of judging others, we judge ourselves far more harshly. Take an inventory of your own great qualities that are present no matter what you look like. Remember, these are the qualities that will be with you if you live to be one hundred. They are your real treasure. Cultivate them now.

83 WHY AM I SO RELUCTANT TO FACE REALITY?

I wish I had a nickel for every time I uttered the phrase, "Maybe it will go away." Sometimes "it" does go away, but often it does not. It's just a case of wishful thinking. I know that waiting usually only causes things to worsen, but I hope that my problems will go away by themselves. While logic points in the right direction, I continually adopt the "maybe it will go away" philosophy.

I T IS NOT AN EXAGGERATION to say that your life would be much easier if you didn't try to hide from the truth. But you prefer to wait until other aspects of your life improve so you are better equipped emotionally to handle a crisis. This thinking helps make you king of the procrastinators. You don't want to start any project or do anything that might lead to a problem or an inconvenience. You don't want to "uncover" anything that may lead to more stress in your life. There's no room for any more worry. Since all change causes stress to some degree, the status quo is what you shoot for. Ironically, the harder you try to avoid stress, the more you take on. This is because isolating yourself from your world diminishes your ability to control your environment and circumstance. This powerless feeling feeds on your anxiety, while you continually wonder, what will happen to me next? You would love nothing more than for everything to remain as it is. Sometimes unpleasant things do go away, but most of the time they do not. If anything, they usually get worse. Yet you cling to the possibility that your problems will go away. Your thinking is immature, and you convince yourself that if you just ignore something long enough it will be okay.

The following scenario illustrates this mentality. You're sitting alone in the back of a moving bus. You suddenly realize that the driver has fallen asleep at the wheel. There are two distinct responses to this scenario, but you would be more inclined to brace yourself for impact than to run to the front to try to take control of the bus. The latter is riskier because you can be hurt more seriously if you crash before you reach the steering wheel. But it's also the only way you can avert a crash. You are too eager to let things happen around you, only to bear the consequences of your inaction.

 **Whenever you are faced with a challenge that you are inclined not to deal with, stop and write down exactly what you believe the problem is.** Often we don't feel we can deal with something because it's too vague. We don't clearly conceptualize it in our own mind, and it's pretty difficult to fight a cloud! The clearer you can get about your situation, the better.

 **Connect to the dire consequences of not taking action immediately.** Ask yourself, "What is the potential for disaster if I don't address this problem right now?" "If I let this situation continue at work, how will it harm my career?" "If I don't change the way I relate to my significant other, how miserable will I be?" "If I continue spending more than I make, how long before I am so far in debt that I'll have to declare bankruptcy and will never be able to get credit again, in addition to being totally disgraced?" Make the consequences of not acting as painful as possible.

Then ask yourself, "What will my life be like if I handle this problem right now?" How much more successful will you be? How much happier will you and your significant other be in your relationship? How much relief will you feel to be completely debt free, with a nest egg to cover any eventuality? Connect to the great feelings that will arise once you take action and handle your problem rather than postpone it.

3 Make a list of five actions you can take immediately to solve the problem or improve the situation. These solutions don't necessarily have to transform the problem all at once, but they should definitely have the potential to make the situation better. Then, before you do anything else, take one of those five actions immediately. You want to train your brain to see the problem and then take action.

For example, if the problem is, "My partner and I are not as close anymore. Our relationship is no longer as warm and loving as I'd like it to be," here are five potential action items. (1) Send flowers and a note to your significant other. (2) Set up a date night. (3) Make a list of everything you think is great about your partner and leave it for her to find. (4) Call your partner for no other reason than to say, "I love you." (5) Arrange a time to sit down with your partner and ask him to tell you two things he loves about you and one thing he wishes you would change. And you do the same for him. Then each of you commits to doing more of the things the other loves and eliminating the things the other hates. At the end of a week, sit down and report on your partner's results. If you've both been successful in doing more of what the other person loves and doing less of what he or she hates, repeat the process with something new.

Continue taking action to solve your problem until it is handled. Keep adding to your action list as the situation evolves. Make sure you take at least one action every day and congratulate yourself every time you take an action that will solve your problem. You are now in the driver's seat, rather than hiding in the back of the bus. Enjoy the feeling!

84 WHY CAN I TAKE ON THE WORLD SOME DAYS, AND OTHER DAYS I CAN BARELY GET OUT OF BED?

Some mornings I wake up feeling so alive and excited that I feel nothing can stop me. Other times I hit the snooze bar five times and curse the world as I drift off to sleep. Some days seem to drag on forever, while other days fly by.

WHILE EVERYONE HAS BAD DAYS, your energy level constantly goes up and down. Your mood is like a yo-yo. This can be a painfully frustrating way to live. You don't know if or when your energy will suddenly deplete itself and leave you physically and mentally drained. Several factors can contribute to this response. Sometimes a chemical or food allergy can cause sudden mood swings. However, it's more likely this behavior has a psychological rather than a physical cause.

What is this ever-elusive force called energy? The formula for energy is excitement and enthusiasm, directed and focused toward a single passion. When you're excited about something, you find that you have boundless energy. Conversely, when you're not looking forward to something or you're in a hopeless situation, you feel drained and listless. You just want to pull the covers over your head and stay in bed all day. Without a focus your mind is free to wander. This constant churning and turning of random thoughts is what uses up your energy. The more you work toward something, the more excited you are about it, the more energy you have. Conversely, the less specific your agenda the more drained you become. Mental energy can't be stored up. It feeds on itself. It's created out of enthusiasm and passion.

1 **Make sure you have a clear, focused passion in your life, something you are excited about.** Write your passion in one or two sentences, in language that is emotionally powerful for you. Once you've got the words exactly the way you want them, put this statement on five small cards and have them laminated. Put one card right next to your bed so you see it as soon as you wake up. Put another on your bathroom mirror. Post the third on your refrigerator, the fourth on the visor of your car, and the fifth at your desk. Keep this reminder of your passion, your purpose, your reason for getting up, in front of you continuously throughout the day.

2 **Plan something special to look forward to each day.** It can be something simple, like a workout, a special meal, a book or newspaper, or making a phone call to a friend. Knowing you have a fun objective awaiting you will help you bound out of bed with much more energy!

3 **Use a time management system to schedule your projects and your free time.** You can't put a dent in infinity. When your objectives are vague, your motivation becomes stifled. Too often our energy dissipates if we either feel we have too much to do or find ourselves with "holes" of time during the day where we don't know what to tackle next. Both of these situations can create a lack of mental focus. When you have a plan for your day, with certain objectives and time lines clearly established, you're much more likely to be focused and more productive as a result. You feel much more energy when you know clearly where that energy's going!

85

WHY DO I FEEL THE NEED TO COMPARE MYSELF WITH OTHERS?

"I'm taller than you and shorter than her." "You've got a nicer car, but you don't drive as well as I do." "I do better work on a good day, but he is more consistent." "Your lasagna is good, but you've got to try my baked ziti." "I can't tell jokes well, but I've got a better sense of humor." And on and on and on.

OUR SOCIETY IS STRUCTURED AROUND a "norm." Everything we do in life is usually judged in comparison to something else. From psychology to medicine to engineering, comparison forms the basis for evaluation of everything—all people, places, and things. We judge everything—from our behavior, success, weight, height, to appearance—according to an established and ever-changing norm. So when it comes to people, it's no wonder you're quick to offer up a comparison as a basis for judgment.

Comparisons provide an opportunity for you to feel better about yourself without having to improve yourself. You don't have to measure your progress based on accomplishment. Instead it is based on comparison. Although you are quick to compare yourself with others, you prefer not to compete with them. Competition may be injurious to your ego. You need to be able to pick and choose whom and what you are measured against. In this way you can ensure the outcome that you want. If you want to feel good about yourself, you need only find someone worse off. If you feel like being self-deprecating, you find someone who is doing better than you.

Comparison also allows you to justify your own behavior, which you might otherwise have difficulty rationalizing to yourself. Having cheated on your husband, you might feel a little guilty. However, when you compare yourself to Mary, who has had six different affairs during her marriage, you don't feel too badly.

Finally, when you feel in a self-deprecating mood, you need only glance at the achievements of another to reinforce your feelings of inadequacy. You get to enjoy the "benefits" of tearing yourself down without ever having to do anything.

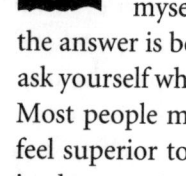 **As soon as you compare yourself to someone else, stop!** Ask yourself, "Am I making this comparison to make myself feel better or worse about my own behavior?" If the answer is better—"He has a nicer car, but I'm a better driver"— ask yourself what's the real emotion that lies behind this comparison. Most people make these kind of comparisons because they need to feel superior to others. And all too often, this masks an underlying inadequacy, or a justification of behavior you wouldn't otherwise be able to condone. The first step to handling the tendency to compare is to reveal the emotional need that lies behind it.

If the feeling you uncover is inadequacy, take a moment to appreciate without judgment what the other person has. Enjoy the fact that he or she has a nicer car, or makes a great lasagna, or has a fantastic body. Then think about the second part of the comparison, the part that deals directly with your own qualities or possessions. **Cultivate a feeling of gratitude for all the gifts and qualities you have in your life.** When you're feeling grateful, it's much harder to be envious of others or to feel either superior or inadequate.

If you discover that you're using comparison to justify unacceptable behavior, it's time to take a hard look at yourself. Ask, "Regardless of others, is this the way *I* want to behave? Is this how

I choose to live my life?" The only one who can set your standards is you, and you're the only one who can ultimately hold yourself to those standards.

3 **Look at your motives.** If the response to the question, "Am I making this comparison to make myself feel better or worse about my own behavior?" is worse, then the feeling you're experiencing is definitely inadequacy and lack of self-worth. Your motivation is to tear yourself down, not to build yourself up. You can handle this in two stages. **First, whenever you compare yourself to your detriment, turn the comparison around by adding, "And what's great about me is . . ."** For example, if your comparison is, "She makes friends so easily, and I can't seem to talk to people," you might add, "And what's great about me is that I really treasure the friends I have." If you say, "They're so successful, and I've been a failure at everything I try," you might add, "And what's great about me is that I keep on trying no matter what!" Finding something great about yourself helps to dissipate the negative feelings of the comparison and gets you ready to make a change.

Second, study the person you're comparing yourself to and ask, "What can I learn from this person that will help me improve myself now?" You can learn something from everyone to apply to your own life. If she's beautiful and you feel you're not, what is it that you really admire in her and what can you learn from her? Grooming? The way she holds herself? How she relates to people? If someone is successful and you feel you've always been a failure, who better to imitate than someone who is doing what you want to do? You have to really take a look at the person and discover what he or she does that you can duplicate, then put those actions into practice in your own life.

86

WHY DO I DO SUCH TERRIBLE THINGS EVEN THOUGH I'M A GOOD PERSON?

I'm a caring and giving person, and at times I put everything on hold to help out a friend. But sometimes I can be cold and calculating. I can think the most horrible thoughts and be driven to be almost abusive and downright mean. I can be manipulative and dishonest, and I'm known for my bad temper and episodes of rage.

L ET IT FIRST BE SAID that even Mother Teresa has her off days. Every once in a while we can all go a little "nuts," saying and doing things we later regret. It's often the case that your stress level just reaches its boiling point. You need to blow off a little emotional steam. However, there is a marked distinction between behavior that's a little extreme and behavior that goes overboard.

Constant shifts in "personality" are indicative of someone who is self-absorbed. You have what can best be described as a conscience by convenience. You can be nice, but only if or when it's convenient for you. Your behavior fluctuates as your needs change. You don't mind helping another so long as it doesn't injure you in any way. You cannot understand why other people think of you as selfish. You think you're the greatest person in the world. All kind deeds take prominence in your memory and all negative behavior is neatly justified with the thinking, *If it's good for me, it's good for everyone.* You often enjoy engaging in what I call comparison by illusion. In other words, you think of something unkind that you "can" do, but choose not to. Therefore you can rationalize what a great person you are. However, just because you don't do a bad thing it doesn't make you a good person.

In more extreme instances you may feel the need to get back at the rest of the world for any actual or perceived injustices perpetrated against you. You feel that you are out for yourself because no one else is looking out for you. The world has been unfair to you, and you seek out happiness and pleasure regardless of the cost.

You may consider yourself to be a caring and altruistic person, but you cannot give a great deal of attention to yourself and to others simultaneously. If you're preoccupied with the I, there is little room left for the rest of the world. You may go on about the horrors of hunger and homelessness, then get a headache and step over a bleeding man in the street to get an aspirin. You may be concerned with the well-being of others only when you are comfortable and secure. These feelings of altruism quickly give way to self-absorption when you yourself are in pain.

When people act cruelly they do so because they're angry and frustrated. Have you ever noticed the way fights break out at basketball games or other sporting events? They're rarely initiated by members of the winning team. Why? Because they're not the one's who are frustrated. It's the team that's losing that acts out. Your unkind actions are motivated by the gnawing feeling that you're losing in the game of life. It's for this reason that when you're in a good mood you are kinder—because you don't feel frustrated.

1 **Whenever you take an action, always ask three questions.** *"What is the effect of my behavior on others?"* Recognize that on an *emotional* level, everything you do has an impact on someone else. Asking this question takes your focus off of your own needs and raises your awareness of the consequences of your actions on others.

"Does this behavior represent the person I want to be?" Often the negative behavioral choices we make are a response to the circumstances of the moment. If we take a minute to remember the kind of person we want to be, we will make another choice.

"What is the effect I want to have, and how will it benefit all parties involved?" You need to make sure your brain has another option available in the moment, one that will produce a positive effect for both you and the other person.

2   **If you find yourself acting out of anger, take a time-out to investigate what you're really angry about.** Often we direct our anger inappropriately, toward people we feel can't or won't hit back. First, take a moment to step back and cool down. Second, ask yourself what's really going on here. What's the emotion underlying your actions? Are you angry, upset, disappointed, or hurt? And what is it about? Cruel or hurtful thoughts or actions can arise from many sources. Once you've uncovered the true underlying emotions, you can deal with them more effectively than by acting them out in inappropriate ways.

3   **Make it a practice to consistently put the needs of others before your own.** Give someone your place in line. Ask someone else what movie to see, or let him or her pick the restaurant. Go to your in-laws' for the holidays. Give a coworker a greater share of the credit for a project you worked on together. Get into the habit of being emotionally generous with other people. You're training yourself right now to consistently be the good, helpful person you are part of the time!

87 WHY AM I SO PARANOID?

I hear people laughing and talking as I walk by, and I'm convinced that the conversation is about me. If it rains on the day of my picnic, I think that the world is out to ruin my plans. At some level I know this thinking is irrational, but I really do think that bad things happen to me deliberately. I expect the worst to happen, and I am always jumping to conclusions and reading into things. I don't like to let people see my true self because I don't want them to use anything they learn against me.

THE WHOLE WORD IS OUT to get you, or at least that's the way it seems to you. There are aspects of yourself that you dislike, and you project your own disdain of these qualities into the minds of other people. You believe, albeit unconsciously, that others must see these faults and dislike you as well. You assume a transparency whereby your faults are on display for the rest of the world to see and criticize. This assumed transparency is magnified by a sense of guilt. Not only are your faults on display, but guilty feelings make your misdeeds take center stage for the world to see.

This makes you extremely sensitive and fragile because you always feel you are on the defensive. Any action by another can be interpreted as an assault on you. You can't stand the fact that someone might be thinking ill of you. You never assume the blame in arguments or disagreements because you're in constant defense of your ego and cannot bear the brunt of even the slightest assault to it. You can become hostile and uncooperative. You feel that you can never let your guard down, because others may try to take advantage of you.

If in the past you were too trusting and were taken advantage of, your paranoia is the result of a rebound effect. You go from totally open and exposed to guarded and cautious. It's a defense mechanism employed to avoid the pain of being too open and trusting.

You want to make absolutely sure that no one ever takes advantage of you. This causes you to be confrontational over prices of items you purchase. You don't want anyone to think of you as foolish or dumb. So you go to the other extreme of haggling, even over the smallest of details in a negotiation.

When you find yourself thinking that other people are talking about you or the world is against you, repeat your new mantra, "It's not about me. It's not about me. It's not about me." Then take a moment and realize how ridiculous your fears are. Do you really think you're so important that everyone in the world is concerned with you? Develop a sense of humor about yourself and your fears. If you can gently laugh at yourself, you've come a long way to developing a healthier perspective on the world and your relation to it.

If you find yourself becoming defensive because of the way you're interpreting the words and actions of others, stop, take a moment to breathe, repeat the mantra, and then ask yourself, "What else could this mean?" This powerful question will open your mind to other interpretations of people's behavior. If it's not about you, and if there is another way to view someone's actions or words, you have the space to relax and view the situation accurately. You're not simply reacting to others; you are in control.

Every time you find yourself expecting the worst, ask yourself, "What's the best that could happen in this situation?" Take a few moments to let your imagination run wild and come up with the most outrageous positive result you can. (If you're used to looking on the dark side only, this may take a little practice. You should feel like you're the world's biggest cock-eyed optimist when you answer this question!) **Then ask yourself, "What's the realistic outcome of this situation?"** You don't want to be an optimist or pessimist either; what you're seeking is the happy medium that allows you to take all factors into account and come to a logical conclusion.

Choose someone you feel somewhat close to and share a feeling or thought with him or her that you would tend to keep to yourself. Notice that person's response to you and how it makes you feel. Your goal is to get into the habit of being more open about the thoughts and feelings you previously hid because you were afraid of the reaction. The secret is to start small, with people you can trust. You will learn that you can share what's going on with you, good and bad, and people can be sympathetic, open, and helpful. Instead of keeping people at a distance, you'll discover that you can use discernment to develop quality relationships that will enrich your life.

88 WHY DO I FEEL NOBODY REALLY KNOWS OR UNDERSTANDS ME?

I feel most people have the totally wrong impression of me. They think I'm fragile when I'm really strong, or uninteresting when I'm actually a brilliant conversationalist. I feel people don't often show me the respect that I deserve. If they really knew me, they would treat me much differently. I believe I could do and be so much more if I were just given the opportunity to show what I'm really capable of. I constantly feel misunderstood, in part because I have trouble communicating my ideas and thoughts. I usually feel that people entirely miss my point in conversations or arguments. Sometimes I feel like I must be from another planet.

I'T'S LIKELY THAT YOUR ACTIONS do not accurately reflect your thoughts. You're not living the kind of life that you would like to be living, and you aren't doing the things you would like to do. Therefore, other people are not seeing the real you. You're being judged by your behavior, when you would prefer to be judged by your intentions, visions, and ideas.

You believe that others are not able to see the barriers that exist for you. You're doing as well as you possibly can, "considering the circumstance." There's a comfort in believing that no one is aware of your problems and troubles and that you're simply misunderstood.

If you felt that other people *did* understand you and didn't like you, it would be devastating. This thinking provides comfort and an explanation for others' lack of appreciation for you. As the saying goes, "To know me is to love me." In other words, "People don't like me; therefore, they must not really understand me." Instead of facing the reality that not everyone will love you, you'd rather assume that they just don't know you well enough.

In a way, you really don't want to be understood. It's in this isolation that you find your uniqueness. Being understood and a part of it all makes you feel ordinary and average. Your self-worth is based almost entirely on your uniqueness. You need to believe that not being understood means that you are a *one of a kind*. What other explanation could there possibly be?

 **In your journal or on a piece of paper, answer the question, "Who am I?"** Include in this description every trait you feel you have, your strengths, your weaknesses, your beliefs about yourself and other people, your interests, your work, your relationships—everything you can think of that describes who you are. When you're finished, review your list. Highlight everything you want to focus on, every trait you would like to develop further, everything you feel is important to emphasize when you're communicating who you are to others.

On a separate piece of paper, write what you think your purpose for being on this planet is. Read this statement over and over again until you're fully connected with it. The combination of this sense of purpose with the qualities you've chosen from your list will give you a powerful sense of identity, one that will help you communicate authentically with others.

As the saying goes, "Who seeks to be understood must first understand." Do you just give up when you feel people don't see you for who you really are, or do you take the time and effort not just to communicate with them but also really to hear what they're communicating to you? If you're feeling misunderstood, it's your responsibility to take the necessary steps to let people know who you really are.

Begin by making sure you truly understand what someone is telling you. Say, "Let me make sure I understand what you're saying. Is it . . ." and then feed back to him what you believe he said. If he agrees, tell him, "I appreciate your thoughts, and my experience is different. This is what's true for me." Said without an emotional "I'm right/you're wrong" charge, these words can open the pathway to clearer communication of your true thoughts and feelings. They also prevents you from misinterpreting what others have to say.

3   **Develop an emotional connection with others.** Communication is a two-way street, and the potential for misunderstanding and misinterpretation will always be there. But if you're connected on an emotional level, you're communicating in a way that goes beyond what anyone says or does. People who can easily connect emotionally with others can handle misunderstandings, because their relationships aren't based in the mind, but in the heart.

89 WHY DON'T I TAKE BETTER CARE OF MYSELF? I'M NOT LAZY!

Emotionally, physically, and spiritually I just don't do the things that would make me feel healthier and be happier. I know that if I did these things I would be glad, but I just can't get over that initial hump. In the past I've broken out of this groove from time to time, but never with any sustained effort.

TAKING CARE OF YOURSELF really means investing in yourself and your future. And investing in tomorrow usually means giving up something today. For example, no sweets now may mean a smaller waistline later. In matters of physical health there is usually one predominant factor that makes this trade-off seem very unappealing.

You don't engage in activities that produce long-term benefits because you are essentially afraid. You're afraid that by improving your lifestyle and physical health you will suffer emotionally. There is an unconscious fear that you will be the one who is left when your family and friends are gone. Being alive longer means it is likely that you will suffer more of this pain. You point to the justification that there are no guarantees in life. Since you might be hit by a bus tomorrow, you might as well enjoy life today. The sad part is that very often you are not even able to enjoy yourself. You may know pleasure, but you rarely know happiness. The activities that you choose are designed for immediate gratification, not for long-term fulfillment.

1 **Develop the muscle of taking action now, instead of putting things off.** Realize that taking care of yourself will give you *a better today* as well as a better future. Like putting your change into a piggy bank and a month later discovering that you have $25 worth of coins, you can invest very little effort, but just the action of doing it every day can produce large cumulative results. Decide what you are going to do to take better care of yourself and make the commitment to take one specific action each day. Do not go to bed until you have taken this action!

2 **Imagine yourself in your old age, sitting in a rocking chair.** How do you feel? What is your level of physical health forty, fifty, sixty, seventy years from now? Are you energized and vital? Or are you filled with aches, pains, and massive infirmities because you didn't take care of yourself when you were younger?

Notice the way you relate to the people around you, whether they're your contemporaries or are younger than you. When you feel healthy, no matter what your age, you're more likely to relate to the people around you in positive ways. Everyone likes to be around healthy, positive people—very few of us like to visit people who are sick, infirm, or just plain miserable! Even if you outlive your friends and family, you can continue to create quality relationships until the day you die. But you're far more likely to create them if you're feeling healthy!

90 WHY DO I EAT FOODS THAT I KNOW WILL MAKE ME SICK?

If it tastes good, I just need to eat it. I know if I eat that extra piece of cake I'm going to feel sick afterward, but I eat it anyway. Spicy foods don't agree with me, and although I might be sick for hours, I nonetheless indulge my craving.

M OST OF US ARE GUILTY of this behavior every once in a while. It's for this reason, in particular, that many people have such an unusual perception of eating disorders. Those who are obese are seen as lazy, undisciplined, and lacking self-respect. Those who suffer from anorexia are considered to be ill and in need of treatment and our understanding. The reason for this dual perception is that we view eating as something pleasurable. Therefore, to deny yourself this indulgence means that you must be psychologically ill. Pleasure clearly is something that is desired, and pain is something that should be minimized.

For some people the pleasure-pain barometer is off balance. If you consistently and constantly eat, drink, or do anything that you know will make you ill and cause you pain, then there is a problem. On a conscious level you tell yourself that you deserve to indulge every once in a while and remain hopeful you won't feel too bad afterward. But there's much more going on at an unconscious level.

You feel that your life is filled with a lot of pain and that you need to grab pleasures wherever you can. The pain that follows is inconsequential because to you life is filled with pain anyway. There's a sense of uncertainty for the future, and you feel that you might as well get as much pleasure in while you still can. Because of this you are typically a great procrastinator. You are highly likely to put off anything that can potentially bring pain, such as a visit to the dentist. Even though waiting might mean enduring more pain in the future, it is of little concern. You're concerned only with the here and now.

You wait for things in your life to improve before you are willing to endure any discomfort in the present. The rationale is that with enough enjoyable and positive influences in your life, you'll be able and more willing to accept painful aspects. What ends up happening is that things get worse and worse as you look for pleasures wherever you can find them. All the while you neglect other aspects of your life. This is a sure fire way to have your life spiral out of control. When your life becomes too unbearable, you may turn to drugs, alcohol, and even suicide. After time, on some level you may begin to realize that this behavior is detrimental. But instead of ceasing it, you may continue with an increased tenacity because you want to punish yourself for having been so neglectful.

1 **If you're a great procrastinator, put off eating!** Take a time-out before you dive into indulging in this particular food. Think of how you'll feel several hours from now, having eaten this and feeling sick as a result. Really think about the food's aftereffects rather than the pleasure you thought you were going to get in the moment. Then, if possible, throw away the food that's tempting you or make another choice quickly, and *leave the vicinity of the food!*

2 **Create a weekly food plan for yourself.** Sometimes planning what you will eat is helpful in controlling your urges. Make sure there is plenty of variety and good taste in your food choices! When you prepare your meals, either prepare only enough for that one meal, or prepare the regular amount and, before you sit down to eat, put the extra into the freezer immediately!

That way, if you have the urge to overindulge, you'll have to take the time to defrost the food before you eat. (No fair using the microwave!)

When you eat, appreciate the tastes and textures of the food you've chosen. Remember that food is designed not to be primarily an emotional satisfaction but rather nourishment for the body. How good does it feel to provide your body with food that supports it rather than makes you sick?

Make an investment in yourself. Each day do one thing that will benefit you in the future. It can be anything from skipping one dessert to cleaning your home. As soon as you begin to take an interest in tomorrow, you'll feel better about yourself today. These simple actions send the message to your unconscious that you like who you are and you want to make your future the best place to live that you can.

91

WHY DO I OVERANALYZE THINGS TO DEATH?

I can't let anything go without a thorough think-through. Everyday things that other people don't think twice about become the focus of my attention. From a two-minute conversation to the design of a building to the writing on a sugar packet, I analyze it all. I like to figure out how things work and how and why they were built or exist.

Y OU SPEND HOURS "working things out" in your mind. You believe that any problem can be solved if you give it enough attention and thought. Your motto is, Everything must have a logical solution. You get in the habit of thinking everything through, whether or not it is of consequence. This leads to the habit of dwelling insatiably on almost anything, which creates a clear path for obsessive behavior. Your need to think things through comes from a fear of making a mistake. You worry that you will miss something if you don't thoroughly examine the facts. When you don't have the answers you need, you take to filling in the gaps by assuming missing information.

You have a need to understand everything, and you hate to miss out on anything you think may be important. You can spend hours going over conversations in your head. You often imagine yourself in impossible situations and then try to figure out how to get out. You don't like magic unless you know what the secrets are. A puzzle or mystery with no answer is a surefire way to drive you crazy.

1   **The next time you begin to analyze something, repeat to yourself, "It's okay for me to not know."** Not everything needs to be examined and turned inside out. There's something to be said for taking things at face value. Explore in depth only those things that give you pleasure to do so.

2   **Develop an appreciation of the magic the universe has to offer.** When you were a child, how much fun did you have playing games in which there was mystery and magic and you didn't know what was going to happen? There are times when it's appropriate to investigate the fine points—when you're developing a financial plan, for example—times when it's unnecessary—when you're on vacation, working on a hobby, or attending a magic show—and times when it's actually detrimental—in most of your intimate relationships! Ask yourself, "Do I really have to know all the details, or can I just sit back and enjoy the ride?" Allow yourself to relax and connect to your emotions rather than to the frantic activity of your mind. It's not your responsibility. You don't have to know everything.

3   **Spend five minutes in quiet reflection.** Everybody is busy, running and racing around. And there's nothing more important to your mental health than this step. Take five minutes out of your day. Sit quietly without music or any other external distraction. Think about whatever you wish, but have no special agenda. These five minutes, you will find, may be the most rewarding time of your entire day.

92

WHY DO I PURSUE THINGS I REALLY DON'T WANT?

I've spent and continue to spend much of my life going after things I'm not even sure that I want. I have things in my life I don't really want, and I don't have much of what I do want. After I acquire something or get involved in a new relationship, I wonder what made me think I wanted it in the first place.

Y OU MAY BE BUSY satisfying lesser pleasures at the expense of greater achievements and accomplishments. You are unable to delay gratification of simple pleasure for the long-term investment of a greater goal.

The reason you're spending your life moving in the wrong direction and not following your dreams is that you prefer to rely on society to set the standard of choice. From what to wear, to where to live, to what kind of work to do, others are your barometer. You don't trust your own judgment or taste, so you buy what is expensive, pursue the person who is a challenge, and desire a car whose color is rare. From career, to food, to romance, you make decisions based on what other people value. You rely on the rest of the world to tell you what is valuable rather than make the decision yourself. You operate at this level with most of your decisions. You're quick to abandon your own interests and taste for what other people think is better. You prefer things that are standard, not customized. You may prefer that others do your decorating or designing because you don't trust your own taste and talent.

 **Before you take any major action, ask yourself, "If this purchase, this relationship, this activity, was free and available to anyone and everyone, would I still want it?"** Only if the answer is yes should you take action. Make sure this is something that you really, truly desire with all your heart and not just something that you *think* is valuable.

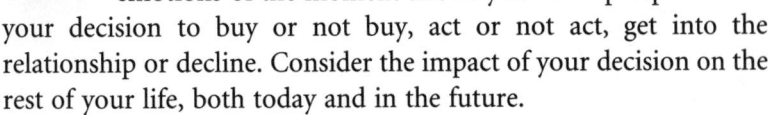 **Evaluate each purchase, relationship, and activity in relation to your greater goals.** Will this move you closer to the life you desire to live and support the purpose and passion you're living for, or is it just a distraction to pull you off course?

If all else fails, wait a day or two before you act. Sometimes taking the time to step back and get out of the emotions of the moment allows you more perspective on your decision to buy or not buy, act or not act, get into the relationship or decline. Consider the impact of your decision on the rest of your life, both today and in the future.

93 WHY DO I DWELL ON THE PAST?

In my conversations and my thoughts, the topics vary but the time frame doesn't. I'm stuck in the past, in the proverbial good old days.

L IVING IN THE PAST provides you with a variety of benefits, the foremost being certainty. (1) The past never changes; it is a constant in a world of uncertainty. Even if you had a terrible childhood, you know that nothing bad can ever happen to you again in the past. You would prefer to live where there is security and predictability as opposed to the future, which is filled with uncertainty. (2) You offer up the past as an explanation to others, and as a justification to yourself, of your current behavior and circumstance. "I am like this today because of what happened . . ." You need an external explanation for your situation. You are not prepared to assume responsibility or blame, so the past becomes your unchallenged scapegoat. (3) The past may be your only source of pride and accomplishment. You need to tell people and remind yourself of the person you *were*. The past may be all that you have left. It's much safer to reminisce about the old days than it is to create new memories.

 **Recognize that although the past can provide you with support, the only one in control of your present and future is you.** And using the past as your only reference limits your ability both to respond to challenges and to get the most out of what life offers you. Remember, those who use only their past as a reference are doomed to repeat the same mistakes over and over again. They're not open to the new solutions and gifts that are present in every moment. Think of how children respond to the world. Do kids live in the past? No way. Children are the ultimate examples of flexibility, joy, and the ability to respond to the world afresh in every moment. Respond to the world as a child, without references to the past, and see how much richer your life can be.

 **If you have trauma in your past that you have been using as justification, ask yourself, "How much more pain am I going to allow this to cause me?** Is this trauma worth the destruction of the rest of my life? Who's in charge here—this trauma or me?" Repeat to yourself, "My past is past; my present is the most important gift I have." Make the decision that you will no longer choose to be affected negatively by your past. From now on, you control how you react to present-day events. Remember, every day you have the opportunity to wake up and start afresh. *Carpe diem*—seize the day!

 **Make sure you're doing something today that you're proud of, that you can talk to others about.** Even if it's seemingly minor, like being consistent at work, or taking care of a pet, or really getting into a hobby, recognize your present-day accomplishments. There's nothing wrong with enjoying your past accomplishments and sharing them with others, but dwelling on them can stop you from continuing to grow. Whenever you find yourself talking about the past, say, "And this is what I'm doing now . . ." You'll find that the present is a great place to be!

94

WHY DO I FEEL SO HOPELESS?

I feel as if I'm doing everything I have to do and I'll never be able to do the things that I really want to do. I often feel tired, disgusted, and fed up. I'm tired of dreaming and fantasizing about how things could be. I don't think there's any way I'll ever reach my goals. I'm in a rut, and it's all I can do to keep my head above water. I'm just not able to get excited about anything anymore.

Y OU HAVE A CONFLICT between where you are and where you think you should be. Feelings of hopelessness arise when you don't think you'll ever be able to get to where you want to be or do what you really want to do. You have hit the proverbial wall and can move no farther. This feeling is compounded when you have to do things you don't want to do. Spending your time on things that you feel obligated to do is draining. So not only can't you do what you want, you have to do things that you don't want to do. This is the formula for hopelessness. With no hope of anything better, and spending your time on things you don't want to do, depression is not far behind. Have you ever noticed how difficult it is when you're in a bad mood to try to act as if you're having a good time? You feel drained, mentally and physically. Or when somebody whom you don't want to speak to calls, you almost feel the energy being drained from you. Imagine how draining it is to live a life you would rather not be living.

You're living in the gap between where you want to be and where you think you should be. Your incentive for working and achieving seems nonexistent. As this feeling continues you may begin to be filled with anger toward yourself as you realize that you are the only one who has been holding yourself back. Afraid to make changes or take risks, you find it harder and harder to justify your behavior to yourself.

 Pick something small that you really want to do and go do it. Choose something at work, a hobby, or a trip; whatever it is, make sure it's something that will give you pleasure. Realize that when you set a goal and take action, you have taken the first step away from hopelessness and toward a vital life. Train yourself to continually set small goals and achieve them. This will give you an ongoing feeling of accomplishment and a sense of power over the course of your life.

Take a dream you have that you really want and feel might be achievable and create a specific, sensible action plan and time line for accomplishing this dream. And take the first step in your action plan within twenty-four hours of creating your plan. Hopelessness is often the by-product of inaction, and vice versa. Don't just do something, do anything! The feeling that you may never get to where you want to be can be erased in a moment. Have you ever noticed that when you take a step toward achieving something that you really want you feel on top of the world? Whether it is joining the gym or sending out your résumé, just moving toward your objective creates a sense of empowerment. It sends the message to your brain that you are in fact in control of your life and your happiness. Simply move in the direction you *want* to go in, and you will naturally move away from the situation you *are* in.

3 **As a part of your action plan, include lots of rewards along the way.** You don't want to wait until you reach your dream to give yourself permission to feel good! When you reach a milestone or meet a deadline, do something to celebrate. The better you feel on a consistent basis, the farther your old feelings of hopelessness will recede and, ultimately, vanish, as you have more and more experiences of creating your dreams.

95
WHY DO I FEEL NUMB AND UNCONNECTED?

Sometimes I feel as if I'm not a part of the world around me. I feel insensitive and callous to everything and everybody. I feel I'm just going through the motions, as if I'm on autopilot. When I get like this, I'm in a fog and can forget the most common things, including my phone number or my best friend's name.

A STATE OF ENHANCED ANXIETY or preoccupation can result in this behavior. In effect, your attention to yourself and to your surroundings is absent. This evokes something similar to absent-mindedness—an absentbodiedness, of sorts.

If this behavior has been integrated into your personality, where this state is easily or constantly induced, then there are other issues and explanations. This state of behavior may be an unconscious defense mechanism. You refuse to acknowledge on a conscious level something in your life that may evoke painful memories, guilt, or any feeling too uncomfortable to look at and deal with. When you are no longer able to suppress or deny these feelings, you disassociate yourself from them.

This detachment does not have to be issue oriented. In other words, you might have had a physical or psychological trauma in the past. In this case, you have shut down your emotions, with a blanketing effect. Nothing comes in, and nothing goes out. You feel that you must protect yourself from ever being injured again.

1 **When you feel disconnected, that's a signal to look outside of yourself.** Change your focus from how you're feeling to what's going on with the people around you. Get curious about what they're thinking and feeling. Ask yourself, "What's great about this person? How can I be of service in this situation? What's the best way to connect with this person's heart?" When you're truly interested in others, you will find yourself naturally becoming more caring, more connected, and more compassionate with others, and then, perhaps, with yourself.

2 **If you feel you're on autopilot, change your routines.** Once again, you want to bring your focus from the inside to the outside, and changing the way you accomplish routine tasks forces you to stay awake and aware. Change the hand you brush your teeth with. Drive to work a different way. Change the order in which you do things—if you make coffee, then get the cornflakes, then pour your orange juice, pour your juice first, then make the coffee, then get a bran muffin instead of cereal. The freshness with which you approach everyday, ordinary tasks provides newness and variety to your actions that can help spark feelings of newness in your emotions as well.

96

WHY DO I CRAVE ATTENTION?

I need to be the center of attention. When I'm not, I get annoyed and bored. I can be very dramatic and love to have the spotlight on me at all times. Sometimes I do things to gain attention, approval, recognition, or compliments, even though they may be a little inappropriate.

YOUR NEED FOR ATTENTION comes from the desire to be recognized and appreciated. The source of this behavior can usually be traced back to childhood. It is there where you felt unappreciated, overlooked, or even abandoned.

You will do just about anything to gain recognition or to call attention to yourself. You may be known as the "clown" or the "wild one." Your true personality takes a back seat to the person you need to become in order to garner the attention you crave. When your emotional void is temporarily filled, you may become a completely different person, because your need to employ dramatics is absent. When your ideas are not taken seriously you become frustrated and belligerent. Your opinions are a reflection of you, and to ignore them is to ignore you.

1 **Treat yourself as if you were your own hero.** When you start to become more "visible" to yourself, you won't be so desperate for the attention of others in order to confirm your existence. You'll already have a solid sense of who you are and what you bring to the world.

Get clear on your own needs and wants, and start meeting them. When you listen to yourself, you won't feel obligated to shout your needs to the world. Do things for no other reason than that *you* want to do them—whether it's taking a bubble bath, test-driving that Corvette you've had your eye on, taking gourmet cooking lessons, or designing the house of your dreams.

Give yourself a "ticker tape" parade, just as if you were a triumphant astronaut returning from the moon. Find video clips or sound effects that will help you get in the mood and throw a big party for yourself. (It would be a good stretch to ask your friends to join with you on this. Tell them you want to do this instead of the obligatory birthday party this year. They might like the idea so much they'll want to do the same thing for themselves!) Fill balloons with helium, throw confetti and streamers around, play the theme from *Rocky* and other triumphant, upbeat music—have a blast! And have someone film the event, so you can look at the pictures every day and remind yourself of what a hero you are.

2 **Create a scrapbook commemorating significant events in your life.** Give this project the same attention you'd give to creating a scrapbook for the president of the United States. Find pictures of yourself through the years, all the way from infancy on up. *What you are doing is celebrating your own history.* Throw your imagination to the winds. Anything and everything is raw material for this scrapbook: drawings from school, love notes, treasured rocks or seashells or feathers, baseball cards, concert tickets, your first canceled rent check, the fraternity pin from your college days.

Decorate the outside of the scrapbook so that just the sight of it fills you with pride. **Don't stop with your past; fill the pages with**

pictures representing your goals and desires. These are an important part of what makes you special and distinctive, so naturally these have a place in your scrapbook.

As an alternative or an add-on, create an audiotape filled with inspiring music and narration about some of the most exciting, fun things you've ever done. Go for it! Give yourself the attention you deserve, and you will always have this wonderful validation to fall back on.

97 WHY AM I SO SENSITIVE TO REJECTION?

I'll do anything to avoid being rejected. I'm hesitant to speak my mind for fear of someone not liking my opinion or ideas. I never approach anyone for fear of being personally rejected. I always make sure I even hang up the phone first at the end of a conversation; otherwise I feel as if I'm being hung up on. As silly as it sounds, it really hurts.

Y OU DON'T FEAR REJECTION of yourself as much as you fear rejection of the image you have of yourself. Rejection of any kind brings into question your opinion of yourself. If someone doesn't like your idea, you wonder if you're stupid. If someone doesn't like your shirt, you wonder if you have bad taste. If someone breaks a date, you wonder if you're unlikable.

Your feelings of inadequacy are compounded by your tendency to see things in black and white. For you there is no gray. In a disagreement someone must be right and someone must be wrong. Therefore you are quick to become defensive. You allow little possibility for the idea that there is such a thing as misunderstandings and miscommunications.

Your own opinion of yourself is so fragile that you cannot risk questioning your self-worth. It's for this reason that you may end relationships prematurely and even fear getting involved in the first place. You cannot bear the brunt of rejection, so you avoid any situation that may lead to it.

You are highly sensitive to criticism because you are not able to receive it in perspective. Any aspect of yourself that is brought in to question brings your entire self-concept into doubt. The reason you get offended is because someone has pierced your shell. A truth that you acknowledge does not offend, nor does a lie that you know to be false. Only a truth that you don't want to recognize as such causes you pain.

Get up in front of people and debate a position that is the exact opposite of what you believe. Talk about leaping from the frying pan into the fire! It takes guts to do this and the next couple of assignments, but few methods are more effective at rapidly building self-confidence.

Find a group that gives you a context for doing this process: a public speaking group such as Toastmasters International or a speech class or debate team at your university extension. Volunteer for exercises in which two speakers must take opposing points of view and have three minutes in which to argue their respective cases. Take the position that you would normally oppose. This will force you not only to explore a perspective from every possible angle (searching for *something* you can argue convincingly) but also to stand up for something, period, and quickly come up with reasons to defend it. The fact that you honestly reject this very point of view and are now defending it will teach you some valuable lessons about thinking on your feet. You will learn *and feel* that when someone disagrees with you it does not mean the end of the world. Everyone will know that this is an exercise and that you could just as easily (in fact, more easily) have argued the opposite point of view. And just by "surviving" this exercise, you measurably boost your self-esteem.

2 **"Sell" people something.** It doesn't really matter what you're selling—a product or service for money; an idea, solution, or recommendation you want people to follow— as long as you *put yourself on the line for something you believe.* So find something you can be passionate about and develop a short presentation for your target audience that will absolutely compel them to buy or otherwise do what you want.

Have you found a product you can stand behind, such as a nutritional supplement or a series of books? How about a service— anything from mowing people's lawns to doing their taxes? Do you have a great idea on behalf of the environment or cancer research or consumer advocacy, something that requires the donation of funds and energy from the people you're approaching? Whatever it is, prepare your speech and any visual aids you'll need and decide whether you'll request their help as a group or individually.

Some people will be only too happy to grant your request. Some will want to think about it, in which case persistence can certainly pay off. And some people will turn down your request. That's called rejection, but hey, life has no guarantees, right? You'll never know unless you ask. Keep things in perspective, and remember that some- one who says no this time may say yes the next time you ask. People have all sorts of reasons for deciding not to buy, many of which have *absolutely nothing* to do with you—so don't take rejection personally. Just accept it as a valuable reality check and move on.

98 WHY AM I SO LAZY?

I lack motivation to do pretty much everything and anything. Unless I'm really interested in something, there's no way I can do it. Most things in general don't really interest me anyway. I just don't seem to be able to generate a passion for anything.

M ANY FACTORS CAN contribute to your so-called laziness. A lack of passion can certainly inhibit your drive. If you're not moving toward something that excites you, it's difficult to sustain your efforts.

There are many who believe that there is no such thing as *lazy*. And they are correct—for the most part. Someone who is disabled, or physically challenged, is not called lazy when he or she cannot participate in a certain sport. Similarly, someone who is *psychologically* challenged should not be deemed lazy. Restrictions on the mental abilities prohibit the pursuit and accomplishment of certain goals. Capability does not always mean ability. And ability does not always mean mobility. A lack of mental energy can leave you so drained that you have little ability to focus your efforts. If you're consumed by worries and fears, your mental abilities can be grossly impaired.

Very few of us are lazy when it comes to eating our favorite food. We wouldn't say, "You know I'd love to eat this right now but that fork just looks so heavy." Feeling unmotivated just means that you have nothing to do that really excites you. It's not a matter of discipline as much as your level of interest.

 **1** **Release suppressed emotion.** Lack of motivation, or burnout, often indicates that you've been holding back a lot of negative emotion such as anger, fear, or frustration. Because strong emotions are considered socially unacceptable, we're trained to stuff them deep inside. The problem with this, of course, is that it slowly drains our energy, and eventually we can become so out of touch with ourselves that we don't even know how we feel about things anymore!

Go someplace private, relax, and take several deep breaths. Think about your goals and about the activities that currently fill your life. What emotions come up? Sadness? Fear? Regret? Jealousy? Anger? **Express these feelings now.** Unexpressed emotion is like a poison that slowly drains you. *Let yourself feel the emotions, whatever they are, so you can begin to work them out of your system.*

2 **Find compelling goals and structure your life around them.** You've read many assignments throughout this book that assist you in defining your vision. Here's another one: **Answer the question, "If money and time were no object, what would I be doing with my life?"** Then, *without stopping to think or second-guess yourself,* write down everything—and I mean everything—that comes to mind for the next fifteen minutes. Would you be married or single? In what part of the country—or world— would you be living? What would your hobbies and pursuits be? How would you be earning income?

After you have all these goals written down, review them and select the ones that are absolutely the most important to you. *Which of these goals, if you don't meet them, will cause you to feel as if your life has been a total waste?* It's that level of intensity that will drive you. Maybe you will find several such goals; maybe you will find one. **For each of these priority goals, create a visual or audio representation (a poster or a tape) that you can use every day to plug you back in to your life's purpose.** With a clear sense of what's most important to you and where you're headed, a sense of structure emerges in your life. You'll find yourself doing things that automatically support the attainment of your goal, and with a reason for doing them your laziness dissipates and your energy builds.

99 WHY DO I FEEL MORALLY SUPERIOR?

I know what is right and what is best, and I don't hesitate to let my opinion be known. I feel that many people are misguided, while I stand on firm moral ground.

I F YOU'RE A PERSON OF HIGH MORAL caliber and live an honest, pure life, then you are a rare and noble individual. However, if your actions differ greatly from your ideals, then it's indicative of several factors.

If your moral fortitude is selective in nature, you may have what can best be described as *virtue by cowardliness*, whereby your moral stance is dictated by the fact that you're simply afraid to act on what it is that you really want. Therefore, you declare it morally reprehensible as a means of freeing yourself of the need to face your fear.

Your high moral stance may be an attempt to compensate for feelings you are uncomfortable with and do not want to face. If you are feeling hatred, envy, jealousy, or any other negative emotion, instead of looking at how you feel and dealing with it, you unconsciously balance things out by being exceptionally kind or altruistic.

You don't want to look too closely at who you are. Instead, you wrap yourself in a cloak of virtues and ideas of moral perfection. It's much easier to cling to what is just and right than it is to change who you are.

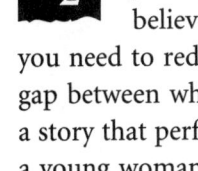 **Face your feelings.** It's wonderful to be kind and helpful, but if you're doing it to cover up feelings you won't admit having, then your altruism is likely to build resentment—and resentment eventually explodes.

First, realize that you're human. You don't have to be the saint of the century; no one's expecting that of you. Are you still carrying over feelings from childhood that someone *is* demanding that of you? **Imagine that you're standing face to face with this person now and tell him or her, "I am not a saint; I am a wonderful human being who's learning and growing better, day after day."** Repeat this process as often as you need until the burden has lifted.

Next, express your emotions in ways that don't hurt you or anyone else. Many examples have been given throughout this book, such as using a punching bag to release your anger. Now there, don't you feel better? Doesn't it feel good to be a human being again?

Review your values and beliefs. Is the high moral ground you stand on really consistent with what you actually believe, or is it a holdover from the past? If the latter, then you need to redefine your moral stance so there is not such a wide gap between what you practice and what you preach. I once heard a story that perfectly illustrates this: During a sermon one morning, a young woman proclaimed that while she strayed from the teachings of the Bible during the week, she was faithful to them on Sunday. The minister, with his usual wisdom, responded, "Ma'am, a religion that's no good on Monday ain't no good on Sunday."

If your beliefs don't support you in reaching your ideals, then you always feel that you don't quite measure up—and you're likely to view other people as falling short, too. *Don't confuse high moral standards with self-righteousness.* If you feel that you're doomed to failure anyway, then you're more likely to think, *Why bother being good at all?* Don't let that happen—give yourself a code you can actually live by, one that will guide you in your daily life.

3 **Talk with someone you trust, such as a priest, minister, rabbi, counselor, or close friend, about ethical issues that are important to you.** All of us are facing the same basic issues. When you consult someone who daily witnesses the broad spectrum of human experience, such as a priest, it provides you with a healthy dose of comfort and self-validation. Don't isolate yourself; share your concerns with others. It's a wonderful relief to get your feelings off your chest and to find out that you're not alone.

100 WHY AM I SO CLOSED-MINDED?

I think in terms of absolutes. Everything with me is black or white, and I'm told I can be very inflexible. I'm quick to make up my mind and slow to change it. When I have a belief about something or make a decision, I refuse to rethink my position despite over-whelming evidence that I am wrong.

B EING A PERSON OF STRONG CONVICTION is certainly not a bad thing. As the saying goes, "If you stand for nothing, then you will fall for anything." However, if the facts are always changing and your opinion never does, then your single-mindedness may be more of a matter of closed-mindedness. To this end, there are two issues at work. First, a need for security and continuity may cause you to attach yourself to beliefs and ideals. You seek some sense of permanence to ground you because you feel unstable and psychologically insecure. Second, you need something to identify with. It's with this identification that you seek to give yourself an identity of your own.

Reluctance to change your mind once you have made a decision is a result of this very identification. Changing your mind is threatening to your ego. Questioning your beliefs in essence causes you to

question yourself and who you are. This is not something you want
to do.

Define who you are. Everyone has an identity, and so do
you—you just need to strengthen your internal sense of
what it is. So here's a fun exercise to lock you right back
on target. **Pretend that an extraterrestrial has just walked up to
you and asked, "Who are you?"** Pretend further that this militant
little creature has stipulated that you must talk *for at least an hour*;
otherwise he'll conclude that the human race is colossally boring and
must be eliminated at once. What will you say?

Write, or talk into a tape recorder, as long as you can. Go as
deep as you can. Aside from all the obvious vital statistics, what can
you add that makes you come alive as a living, breathing, three-
dimensional human being? What stories from your childhood can
you relate? What thoughts occupy your day? Who are your favorite
heroes and fantasy figures, and what does that say about you? How
do you want to make a difference for all future Earthlings yet to be
born? *Make that alien feel perfectly jealous that he wasn't born on
Earth!* If you run out of things to say, start talking about who you
want to be, making sure the E.T. understands how important vision
is to the human race!

Practice the art of flexibility. I've always found it amusing
that people with closed minds are reluctant to let anything
in but at the same are so eager to let everything out—like
their opinions. The sign of an individual who is truly confident and
secure is eagerness to hear new ideas and information and to incor-
porate them into action. With a greater supply of facts and insights,
you don't tear down your identity—you *build* it.

**Today, find out one interesting fact you didn't know, then
come up with a real-life application for it.** For example, let's say
you're an attorney, and the sum total of your knowledge about
oceanography would fill a thimble. Go to your library, or do some
on-line research, and start to educate yourself. Maybe you could find
an application that would have environmental benefits. Who knows,

maybe you could carve out a niche for yourself as an environmental lawyer!

 **See life through someone else's eyes.** There is probably no quicker cure for a case of rigidity than actually going through a whole day from someone else's viewpoint. **Either read a book that presents a completely different viewpoint from the one you're accustomed to or, better yet, find someone who will allow you to "shadow" him or her for a day.** This person could be your spouse (what a great way to gain an understanding of what your mate goes through!), a coworker, your boss, your mother, a friend, a police officer, a stranger, a homeless person on the street.

I predict that after you do this process, you won't be able to look at life in quite the same way again. Not only will you have a deeper appreciation and respect for other people, but you'll have a stronger sense of your own identity as well, and you won't be driven to confuse rigidity with strength. Instead, you'll enjoy the security of being a truly open-minded individual, one who learns and benefits from all that life has to offer.

PART TWO

IT ISN'T OVER YET

T HE FOLLOWING FOUR PHASES are used in conjunction with the responses. They provide four crucial elements necessary for casting aside your facade and allowing you to emerge free and impassioned.

THE TAKEOVER

L ET'S SAY THAT YOU just became president of the largest corporation in the world. Before you took over this company you were not able to make any changes because you weren't working there. As such, there may have been many influences responsible for bringing you to this point in your life—parents, teachers, friends. You can blame anyone that you want for your life up until now. But where you go from here, who you become, is totally up to you. You can only assign blame to those who are in a position of power. And for the rest of your life, the power is yours, and the responsibility that goes with it. You are now in control and responsible for your own life. Your destination, your destiny, is in your own hands.

Now that you're in charge, as president of this company, you're going to make some changes and set new objectives to make it even more successful. The first thing that you may want to do is to take inventory. You're going to want to look at every aspect of the company. The good and the bad. And now that you're in charge of your life, that's exactly what you're going to do here.

Acknowledging who and where you are, your strengths as well as your weaknesses, is the beginning of any growth process. You can't change what you refuse to acknowledge even exists. If you deny who you are, you can't become more than what you are right now. Every time you refuse to acknowledge a truth, you send a damaging message to your unconscious. "I don't like who I am." "Others won't like me if they really know me." And "I am weak and need to protect myself." It actually makes you increasingly psychologically insecure. It's the strong who can acknowledge his or her own weaknesses.

You can't get to point B—your objective—without knowing

where you're starting from, point A. Before you're able to set new objectives for yourself, you need to know what you're starting with. So let's take a personal inventory!

You're going to create a balance sheet on yourself, objectively listing your assets and your liabilities. The purpose here is to see who you are and where you are at this point in time.

1. The things I like most about myself are . . .
2. The things I dislike about myself are . . .
3. My fears are . . .
4. My hopes and dreams are . . .

The act of simply writing this down is so powerful because most people have never objectively looked at themselves and their life. Take a look at your inventory. Now you know where you stand, your physical, spiritual, and psychological starting point.

Take an objective look at your lists. What is on lists 2 and 3 that you want to change? How many of the items on lists 2 and 3 are things that are under your control? For example, can you change everything that you dislike about yourself? Most people will fill their lists with things like "I procrastinate," "I weigh too much," "I have trouble staying in relationships," and so forth. Can you change all of those things? Of course.

There may be some things on your lists that you can't change. You can't change your skin color or ethnic background. You can't change the parents you had. You can't change the events of your past history. You also can't change other people, can you? If your list of fears, for example, includes things like, "I'm afraid this person will reject me if I ask them out," or "I'm afraid my boss won't promote me," can you truly control what other people do? Probably not. But remember what we said earlier: You can always control the way you respond to people or events. You can always control your attitude about your skin color, abilities, or disabilities, and past history. You can't control whether someone chooses to go out with you or wants to promote you. But you can control the way you respond, and your response may actually help to shape events!

An essential part of happiness and inner peace comes from accepting those things that you can't change and recognizing how you can change the way you respond if need be. For each of the items on your list of things you dislike about yourself, and your list of fears, ask yourself:

1. Is this something I can change? (Not that it's easy to change, or that you must change it, but is it something you could change if you wanted to.)
2. If it's something I can't change, how can I respond to it differently than the way I have responded to it in the past? (Take a moment with each of the items you can't change. Make the decision to accept them and move on. Commit to respond to them differently if these dislikes or fears arise in the future.)

WAKE UP
AND SHAKE UP

J UST AS YOU NEED to wake up your mental routine, you need to shake up your physical routine as well. To give you an idea of just how mechanical your life may be, close your eyes and try to picture the face on your wristwatch. Don't look at it! Do you recall whether it has Roman numerals, slashes, or numbers? Do you know what color the face is? If you're like most people, it took some thinking. You have looked at your watch thousands of times, but you never really saw it.

Have you ever rearranged your furniture and noticed how you felt afterward? This often puts many people in a better mood. You come home, see it, and think, *This looks great.* Our mood is often swayed by our surroundings, and changing your furniture temporarily jolts you out of your usual thought patterns. Some people get depressed as soon as they set foot inside the door. This is called a visual trigger. You see something and you instantly go into a conditioned state associated with your environment. You want to break this kind of conditioning. The objective in this phase is to shake up your daily routine and give you a new awareness of ordinary, everyday behaviors; it helps to put you back in touch with yourself and your life.

Interrupting ordinary patterns of behavior breaks the automation chain and allows for more rapid change in other areas of your life.

To help you with this, try this pattern-interrupting exercise. Every day pick one item from each section below. (These are just examples; you may use others that are more suitable to your lifestyle as long as they are consistent with that section. You don't need to make them difficult, just different.) Leave notes for yourself if you like. The purpose is not to test your memory, it's to break patterns.

1. *Throughout the day, pay attention to one aspect of your physical self.*
   - Notice how you breathe through your mouth or nose.
   - Notice the different parts of your body touching your physical environment.
   - Notice the position of your hands when you're resting, sleeping, or walking.
   - Notice the sensation of your feet hitting the ground when walking.
   - Notice how your mouth and lips move as you speak.

2. *Throughout the day, slightly change one of these ordinary behaviors.*
   - Change the order in which you put on your shoes.
   - Use your other hand to pick up the telephone.
   - Wear your watch on the other wrist.
   - Open doors with the other hand.
   - Change the order in which you wash yourself in the shower or bath.

3. *Shake up your environment at work and/or home. Move around or change things that you see every day.*
   - Move your alarm clock to a different nightstand.
   - Move pictures on your desk to the other side.
   - Move a small appliance (toaster, blender) in the kitchen.
   - Move some food around in your refrigerator and on the counter.
   - Set your watch ten minutes ahead.

4. *Observe how you do certain tasks, without changing them.*
   - How you hold your pencil or fork.

- Which foot hits the floor first when you get out of bed.
- How you hold the toothbrush when you brush your teeth.
- How you sit: where your arms, legs, and head are resting.
- The position of your body in bed as you fall asleep.

5. *Do what you don't usually do, and don't do what you usually do.*
   Take small actions that are inconsistent with your usual behavior.
   - Carry your purse on the opposite shoulder or your wallet in a different pocket.
   - Stir your coffee in a different direction (clockwise or counterclockwise).
   - Eat something for lunch that you have never had before.
   - On your day off, do something you've never done before.
   - When drinking, hold the glass with the other hand.

You'll find that this exercise will give you a heightened awareness of the unconscious patterns in your daily routine and will forge a path toward change in all areas of your life.

JUSTIFYING YOUR OLD WAYS

T HE TECHNOLOGY FOR THIS exercise employs a powerful psychological tool. The most basic inherent instinct is of survival. It's our nature to want to stay alive. But there's an instance where this instinct is overridden—intentionally taking one's own life. There are four separate psychological processes involved in "death by decision."

- Committing suicide out of depression or other mental illness
- Taking one's own life because of principles, such as a hunger strike
- Taking one's own life because of external influence, such as cult member suicide
- Giving one's own life to save another

While the motivation in each example is different, they all have one thing in common. The I, or the self, is absent. Physical welfare becomes unimportant and the person's very identity has been transferred to an objective. His *purpose* is who he is. If he is not this, then he is nobody. He would rather die physically than die psychologically. In other words, his life will have no meaning if he lives and sacrifices his principles. The exception is the first example, where the person feels worthless regardless of his or her actions. Nevertheless, this person, too, would rather suffer physical death than be tormented psychologically.

This phase duplicates this psychological process by artificially inducing the same criterion to effect change in behavior and produce dramatic and effective results. With it you can alter, acquire, or discard any specific action or thought pattern. The behavior can be any of the one hundred responses in the previous section, or any other behavior that you want to change.

We employ a powerful technique called Image Identity Transfer. It works with human nature, not against it. This is the only phase where you do not actively attempt to change anything. The technique is a mental exercise designed to engage a thought interruption to promote dramatic change in your thinking.

Even if there's no immediate change in your behavior, there will be an awareness each time. The discomfort is more intense because you will be conscious of it and feel it every time, fostering the intention to cease.

Follow each step and read aloud #5 two times a day, until the behavior is modified.

1. Write a specific behavior to be altered, discarded, or acquired.
2. Write the reason(s) why you have maintained or not maintained this behavior.
3. Write everything it has cost you and what you have missed out on because of it.
4. Write what you will lose if you continue with the present behavior.
5. I use the power of the past to change my future. I went through all that pain (read #3) to get to where I am today. And I will continue to suffer (read #4) unless I decide to (read #1). It will all be a waste if I continue as I have been, but it's an investment of time if I move in this new direction. The only way to justify spending so much of my time doing what was injurious is to take this new course and make a change. Change is a natural progression and extension. Continuation of my old behavior is a waste of time. Even more important, this gives me consistency and security. I can justify my past only by engaging in this new behavior. I've wasted and lost out only if I continue with my old behavior.

I am not the same person I was before. I am not the person

identified with that behavior. I identify with my new behavior only. If I do not move in this direction, I will remain where I am and suffer because of it.

I see that my behavior was only to protect my true self (read #2). Now change is easier because I no longer have an image to protect; the necessity to continue with it has been removed. My old behavior is pointless. It was designed to insulate me, but it has done more damage than good. The only good that can come out of all that I suffered (read #3) is if I now alter my behavior. It's as if I were told to do it at gunpoint, I no longer feel an obligation to continue as I have. I am ready to move on.

JUMP START

Y OU NOW HAVE THE STEPS you need to reach any specific objective that you desire in any area of your life. But the hardest thing about any task is getting started. Objects in motion tend to stay in motion. This is true not only of the physical world but also of ourselves. Once we get started, we're fine, but it's that initial step that seems to be the hardest. So give yourself a boost! This step allows you to jump-start your commitment to achieving your objective.

This simple process will help you create an immediate change in your behavior and will produce dramatic and effective results. You use this process to alter, acquire, or discard any specific action or thought pattern.

This process acts as a boost to move you quickly in your desired direction. It's called Forced Accelerated Acceptance, and it's designed to give you a mental jolt, because it commits you to justifying your behavior.

Every action, whether it's sensible or stupid, produces in us a need for internal justification. We all want to be right. We need to prove to ourselves, for our own psychological security and sanity, that our actions are not dumb or useless, so we do almost anything to justify them.

You are now going to use this need for internal justification to jump-start yourself toward accomplishing your objective. You are going to do something that you would do only if you became fed up and were willing to do whatever it takes. That's the feeling you want to generate.

For example, someone who wants to quit smoking might buy five cartons of cigarettes and then grind them up in the garbage disposal, one pack at a time. Someone who wants to lose weight would clean out the cupboards of all snack foods and go out and join a gym. Someone who wants to make more money might write a postdated check for a sizable amount to his or her favorite charity and send it to a friend with instructions to mail it on such-and-such a date.

What you do needs to be drastic in reason, not in action. It's not what you do that you are forced to justify, but your reason for doing it. I don't recommend that you choose an action that involves a purchase, however. Too often we justify a purchase without taking further action—"I needed it anyway."

Here are a few examples of different kinds of actions you can take to jump-start you on your way to your objective. Use these as a starting point to come up with an action or actions that will be suitable for your objective.

1. Every day for a week, wake up at 4:00 A.M. and stay up for five minutes while doing something toward achieving your objective.

2. Cancel a date with someone. Say that it's because you're working on your objective.

3. Unplug your phone for a day to work on your objective. Or leave a message on your answering machine and don't pick up the phone.

4. Don't speak to anyone for twenty-four hours. Spend that time thinking about your objective or visualizing your success.

Each of these actions forces you to ask yourself, "Why did I do that?" The only justification for your behavior is, "I must really care about my objective. Look what I've done to ensure my success."

CONCLUSION

T HIS BOOK HAS PROVIDED a comprehensive and complete way to discover who you are and why you do what you do. These one hundred behaviors reveal to you the most precious gift of all—yourself.

As you become more aware of yourself and your world, you will feel rejuvenated and more alive than ever before. Enjoy your new life and your new world.

DR. DAVID J. LIEBERMAN is a nationally recognized leader in the field of human behavior and the creator of Neuro-Dynamic Analysis, a revolutionary short-term therapy. The impact from his groundbreaking research and theories has given Dr. Lieberman an international presence, with writings enjoyed around the world from Australia to Asia to Europe. He is a sought-after speaker and lecturer and is a frequent guest of top television and radio programs. Dr. Lieberman holds a Ph.D. in clinical psychology and is a certified and registered hypnotherapist with the American Board of Hypnotherapy. He writes and lectures full time and lives on Long Island, New York.

If you have any comments or would like information about upcoming events and seminars, please contact Dr. Lieberman at the address below:

Dr. David J. Lieberman
P.O. Box 222041
Great Neck, N.Y. 11022-2041

Or visit us on the World Wide Web at:

www.InstantAnalysis.com